INTERMEDIATE WORKBOOK

THE OXFORD

Picture Dictionary

MARJORIE FUCHS AND MARGARET BONNER

Oxford University Press

Oxford University Press
198 Madison Avenue, New York, NY 10016 USA
Great Clarendon Street, Oxford OX2 6DP England

Oxford New York
Auckland Bangkok Buenos Aires Cape Town Chennai
Dar es Salaam Delhi Hong Kong Istanbul Karachi Kolkata
Kuala Lumpur Madrid Melbourne Mexico City Mumbai
Nairobi São Paulo Shanghai Taipei Tokyo Toronto

OXFORD is a trademark of Oxford University Press.

ISBN 0-19-435074-6

Editorial Manager: Susan Lanzano
Editors: Lynne Barsky/Julie Landau/P. O'Neill
Associate Production Editor: Tareth Mitch
Art Director: Lynn Luchetti
Design Project Manager: Susan Brorein
Design and Page Makeup: Keithley and Associates
Art Buyer: Tracy Hammond
Cover Design Production: Brett Sonnenschein
Picture Researcher: Clare Maxwell
Production Manager: Abram Hall
Production Controller: Georgiann Baran
Cover design by Silver Editions

Printing (last digit): 10 9 8

Printed in China

Illustrations, realia, and handwriting by: Gary Antonetti/Ortelius
Design, Craig Attebery, Eliot Bergman, Annie Bissett, Daniel J.
Brown/Artworks NY, Rob Burman, Carlos Castellanos, Mary
Chandler, Jack Crane/Averil Smith, Dominick D'Andrea, Jim
DeLapine, Maj-Britt Hagsted, Pamela Johnson, Claudia C.
Kehrhahn, Keithley and Associates, Mohammad Mansoor,
Karen Minot, Kristin Mount, Conrad Represents/Max Seabaugh,
Stacey Schuett, Carol L. Strebel, Anna Veltfort, Nina Wallace/
Averil Smith, Wendy Wassink Ackison

*The publishers would like to thank the following for their
permission to reproduce photographs:* M. Angelo/Westlight;
Bruce Ayres/Tony Stone Images; Sandra Baker/Liaison
International; Bruno Barbey/Magnum; Bie Bostrom; Rick
Brady/Uniphoto; Mark Burnett/Photo Researchers; Ken
Cavanagh/Photo Researchers; Junebug Clark/Photo
Researchers; W. Cody/Westlight; Laima Druskis/Photo
Researchers; Alfred Eisenstaedt © *Life* Magazine © Time
Warner, Inc.; Leonard Freed/Magnum; Michael Goldman/FPG;
Mark E. Harris © *Life* Magazine © Time Warner, Inc.; Jeff
Hunter/The Image Bank; Helen Marcus/Photo Researchers;
Patti McConnville/The Image Bank; Kunio Owaki/The Stock
Market; Rondal Partridge; Juan Manuel Renjifo/Animals
Animals; Jon Reily/Tony Stone Images; Don Smetzer/Tony
Stone Images; Vince Streano/Tony Stone Images; Superstock;
Telegraph Color Library/FPG; Camille Tokerud/Photo
Researchers

*The publishers would also like to thank the following for
their help:*
p. 121: Microsoft® Word and Microsoft® Excel are either
registered trademarks or trademarks of Microsoft Corporation
in the United States and/or other countries.

Acknowledgments

The publisher and authors would like to thank the following people for reviewing the manuscript as the book was being developed:

Glenda Adamson, Lubie G. Alatriste, Leor Alcalay, Fiona Armstrong, Jean Barlow, Margrajean Bonilla, Susan Burke, Becky Carle, Analee Doney, Michele Epstein, Christine Evans, Lynn A. Freeland, Carole Goodman, Joyce Grabowski, Kelly Gutierrez, Christine Hill, Leann Howard, Hilary Jarvis, Nanette Kafka, Cliff Ker, Margaret Lombard, Carol S. McLain, Monica Miele, Patsy Mills, Debra L. Mullins, Barbara Jane Pers, Marianne Riggiola, Virginia Robbins, Linda Susan Robinson, Michele Rodgers-Amini, Maria Salinas, Jimmy E. Sandifer, Jeffrey Scofield, Ann Silverman, Susan A. Slavin, Peggy Stubbs, Lynn Sweeden, Christine Tierney.

In addition, the authors would like to thank the following people:

Susan Lanzano, Editorial Manager, for overseeing a huge and complex project of which the *Workbooks* were just a part. She orchestrated the entire project without losing sight of the individual components.

Our editors for their hard work and dedication. Lynne Barsky carried out the important initial research and helped develop the manuscript. Julie Landau took over and made further refinements. Patricia O'Neill carefully and thoughtfully examined the pages and art, checking each comma, space, word, and fact for accuracy. Tareth Mitch scrutinized pages and art, making insightful queries and suggestions. We appreciate the unique contributions of all of these people.

Norma Shapiro and Jayme Adelson-Goldstein, authors of the *Dictionary*, and Shirley Brod, editor of the *Teacher's Book*, for meticulously reviewing the manuscript and offering particularly helpful feedback and enthusiastic support.

Eliza Jensen and Amy Cooper, Senior Editors, for looking at the manuscript at important junctures and offering sage advice.

The design team for making us feel welcome at their meetings, and for giving us the chance to see the huge amount of work and creativity they put into the project long after the manuscript had been submitted.

Luke Frances for always being himself. His honesty, spontaneity, and humor make creativity happen.

Rick Smith, as always, for his unswerving support and for his insightful comments on all aspects of the project. Once again, he proved himself to be equally at home in the world of numbers and the world of words.

To the Teacher

The *Intermediate Workbook* and *Beginning Workbook* that accompany *The Oxford Picture Dictionary* have been designed to provide meaningful and enjoyable practice of the vocabulary that students are learning. At the same time, the workbooks supply high-interest contexts and real information for enrichment and self-expression.

Both *Workbooks* conveniently correspond page-for-page to the 140 topics of the *Picture Dictionary*. For example, if you are working on page 22 in the *Dictionary*, the activities for this topic, Age and Physical Description, will be found on page 22 in the *Workbook*.

All topics in the *Intermediate Workbook* follow the same easy-to-use format. Exercise 1 is always a "look in your dictionary" activity where students are asked to complete a task while looking in their *Picture Dictionary*. The tasks include judging statements true or false, correcting false statements, completing charts and forms, speculating about who said what, categorizing, odd one out, and pronoun reference activities where students replace pronouns with the vocabulary items they refer to.

Following this activity are one or more content-rich contextualized exercises, including multiple choice, quizzes and tests, describing picture differences, and the completion of forms, reports, letters, articles, and stories. These exercises often feature graphs and charts with real data for students to work with as they practice the new vocabulary. Many topics include a personalization exercise that asks "What about you?" where students can use the vocabulary to give information about their own lives or to express their opinions.

The final exercise for each topic is a "Challenge" which can be assigned to students for additional work in class or as homework. Challenge activities provide higher level speaking and writing practice, and for some topics will require students to interview classmates, conduct surveys, or find information outside of class. For example on pages 28–29, the Challenge for the topic Life Events asks students to look up biographical information about a famous person, draw a time line, and write a paragraph about that person's life.

Each of the 12 units ends with "Another Look," a review which allows students to practice vocabulary from all of the topics of a unit in activities such as picture comparisons, "What's wrong with this picture?" activities, photo essays, word maps, word searches, and crossword puzzles. These activities are at the back of the *Intermediate Workbook,* on pages 170–181.

Throughout both the *Intermediate* and *Beginning Workbooks*, vocabulary is carefully controlled and recycled. Students should, however, be encouraged to use their *Picture Dictionaries* to look up words they do not recall, or, if they are doing topics out of sequence, may not yet have learned.

The *Oxford Picture Dictionary Workbooks* can be used in the classroom or at home for self-study. A separate *Answer Key* with the answers to both *Workbooks* is available.

We hope you and your students enjoy using these workbooks as much as we have enjoyed writing them.

M.F. and M.B.

To the Student

The *Oxford Picture Dictionary* has more than 3,700 words. This workbook will help you use them in your daily life.

- It's easy to use! The *Workbook* pages match the pages in your *Picture Dictionary*. For example, to practice the words on page 22 in your *Picture Dictionary*, go to page 22 in your *Workbook*.

- It has exercises you will enjoy. Some exercises show real information; for example, a chart showing the top ten fast foods; a bar graph comparing how long different animals live. Another exercise, "What about

you?," gives you a chance to use your own information. You'll find stories, puzzles, and conversations, too.

At the end of each topic there is a Challenge, a chance to use your new vocabulary more independently. And finally, every unit has a one-page summary, called Another Look, in a section at the back of the book. This is a puzzle activity or a picture composition that practices the vocabulary from an entire unit.

Learning new words is both challenging and fun. We had a lot of fun writing this workbook. We hope you enjoy using it!

M.F. and M.B.

Contents

Contents

Contents

10. Plants and Animals

11. Work

12. Recreation

A Classroom

1. Look in your dictionary. **True** or **False**? Correct the underlined words in the false sentences.

                talking

   a. **Picture B:** The student is ~~listening~~ to the teacher.   _____False_____

   b. **Picture C:** The student is pointing to a cassette.   _____

   c. **Picture E:** The student is sitting down.   _____

   d. **Picture H:** The woman is writing on the board.   _____

   e. **Picture I:** The man is closing his book.   _____

   f. **Picture L:** The student is putting away a pencil.   _____

2. Complete the instruction sheets. Use your own information and the words in the box.

close	pencil	listen	notebook	erase	~~open~~	write	point

Name: _____   Date: _____

                                                                  Class:_____

Instructions:

1. ____*Open*____ your picture dictionary to page 91. _____ to the cassette. When
       a.   **b.**

   you hear a word, _____ to the picture.
                              c.

2. _____ your book. Listen again and _____ each word in your _____.
       d.   **e.**   **f.**

   Use a _____. Do not use a pen. If you make a mistake, _____ it.
              g.   **h.**

look at	screen	stand up	talk to

Directions:

1. _____ and find a partner.
       i.

2. _____ the picture on the _____.
       j.   **k.**

3. _____ your partner about the picture.
       l.

3. Complete the classroom inventory. Write how many of each item. (*Hint:* The items are in alphabetical order.) Add another item for **l.**

Classroom Inventory—Room 304

	NUMBER	ITEM		NUMBER	ITEM
a.	1	bookcase	**g.**		computers
b.	0	bulletin boards	**h.**	2	
c.		cassette players	**i.**		markers
d.	1		**j.**		overhead projectors
e.		chalkboard erasers	**k.**	2	
f.		clocks	**l.**		

4. Write about the items that are in Room 304 and the items that are not. Use your own paper.

Examples: *There's one bookcase. There aren't any bulletin boards. There are three cassette players.*

5. What about you? Do an inventory of your classroom or office. Use your own paper.

Challenge   Describe the ideal classroom. What does it have? How many of each item?

Personal Information

1. Look in your dictionary. Match the information with the line on the form.

    a. January 15, 1980   _16_   **d.** Zakarovsky   _____

    b. John Zakarovsky   _____   **e.** 210 Parker Road   _____

    c. 037-22-7982   _____   **f.** 752-4851   _____

2. Circle four more mistakes on this form.

1. TODAY'S DATE: (12 June) 2004   2. SOCIAL SECURITY #: 077 – 22 – 8765
    MONTH DAY YEAR

3. NAME (Please Print): Ann Brown
    LAST NAME   FIRST NAME   MIDDLE INITIAL

4. TELEPHONE: 286-4872   5. SEX: ☐ Male ☑ Female
    (AREA CODE)

6. DATE OF BIRTH: March 1 1981   7. JOB: Stoodent
    MONTH DAY YEAR

8. ADDRESS (Please Print): 92 Adams Street   4
    STREET   APT. #

    Los Angeles   CA   90046
    CITY   STATE ZIP CODE

9. PLACE OF BIRTH: Germany   10. SIGNATURE: Ann Brown
    CITY COUNTRY

3. What about you? Fill out the form with your own information.

1. TODAY'S DATE: _____   2. SOCIAL SECURITY #: _____ – _____ – _____
    MONTH DAY YEAR

3. NAME (Please Print): _____
    LAST NAME   FIRST NAME   MIDDLE INITIAL

4. TELEPHONE: _____   5. SEX: ☐ Male ☐ Female
    (AREA CODE)

6. DATE OF BIRTH: _____   7. JOB: _____
    MONTH DAY YEAR

8. ADDRESS (Please Print): _____
    STREET   APT. #

    CITY   STATE ZIP CODE

9. PLACE OF BIRTH: _____   10. SIGNATURE: _____
    CITY COUNTRY

Challenge   Describe the mistakes in Exercise 2. **Example:** *In number 1, she wrote the day first, not the month.*

1. Look in your dictionary. Complete the notes with the job titles.

Sunnydale School Newsletter	SEPTEMBER/ OCTOBER • 2001

Sunnydale Staff Notes...

a. Welcome, all. It's going to be a great year! *Rita Riggs,* _____Principal_____

b. Seniors—Let's talk about college soon. *Ana Thomas,* _____

c. If you're late, come to the office to sign in! *Thelma Black,* _____

d. Our class will visit historic places around the state. *Dan Rivers,* _____

2. Look at the list of events. Write the names of the places. Use the words in the box.

field	~~library~~	gym	main office	cafeteria	auditorium

Date and time	Event	Place
a. Sept. 24, 2:00	Reading Club	library
b. Oct. 1, 11:00–1:00	Sandwich and Cookie Sale	_____
c. Oct. 15, 7:00 P.M.	Concert: Sunnydale Choir	_____
d. Oct. 23, 2:30	Football Game, Home	_____
e. Oct. 25, all day	Registration for Senior Class Trip	_____
f. Oct. 30, 4:30	Girls Basketball Practice	_____

3. Make words with the scrambled letters.

SCHOOL SCRAMBLE

a. rcakt   t r a (c) k

b. lacsmoors   __ (_) __ (_) __ __ __ __ __

c. erst moro   __ __ __ __ __ (_)(_) __

d. chleabers   __ __ __ __ (_) __ __ __

Make a new word with the circled letters: __ __ __ __ __ __

Challenge   Draw a map of your school. Label the places.

Studying

1. Look at the pictures in your dictionary. **True** or **False**? Correct the underlined words in the false sentences.

   a. **Picture D:** The woman is ~~looking up~~ *repeating* the word.   _____False_____

   b. **Picture K:** The students are brainstorming a list.   _____

   c. **Picture O:** A student is collecting the papers.   _____

   d. **Picture P:** The students are talking.   _____

   e. **Picture T:** The student is checking the answer sheet.   _____

   f. **Picture X:** The student is underlining the items.   _____

2. Fill in the blanks to complete the instructions for the test. Then take the test.

   Review Test

   1. _____Circle_____ the correct words to complete the questions.

      a. (What)/ Who is your name?
      b. When / Where do you live?
      c. How much / How many brothers and sisters do you have?

   2. _____ the word in each group that does not belong.

      a.   small   cold   fast   ~~hello~~
      b.   pen   marker   coach   pencil
      c.   greet   state   city   country

   3. _____ the words in alphabetical _____.

talk	collect	say	discuss	spell	copy
draw	dictate	~~answer~~	help	~~ask~~	share

      _____answer_____   _____   _____   _____

      _____ask_____   _____   _____   _____

      _____   _____   _____   _____

3. Circle the correct words to complete the article.

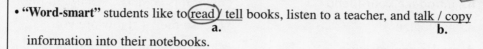

There are many different ways to learn. Which of these match yours?

- **"Word-smart"** students like to (read) tell books, listen to a teacher, and talk / copy
  a.   **b.**
  information into their notebooks.

- **"Body-smart"** learners like to move around. They're often the ones who
  collect / dictate the homework from classmates and circle / pass out papers for the teacher.
  c.   **d.**

- **"Picture-smart"** people draw / repeat pictures to understand new ideas.
                                              e.

- **"Music-smart"** students tap their feet while they learn. They love to repeat / look up
                                                            f.
  information again and again in songs or rhythm.

- **"People-smart"** students need to dictate / talk with others, working in a group to
                                                    g.
  brainstorm / point to a list, for example. They often share / help others in the class.
  h.   **i.**

- **"Feelings-smart"** learners like to discuss / check stories and share / correct their feelings.
                                                 j.   **k.**

In which ways are you smart? Find your style, and make learning fun!

Based on information from: Kennedy, M.: "Finding the Smart Part in Every Child." *Good Housekeeping* (October 1995).

4. What about you? What helps you learn? Check (✔) the columns that are true for you.

ACTIVITY	HELPS ME A LOT	HELPS ME SOME	HELPS ME A LITTLE	DOESN'T HELP ME
Looking up words				
Copying words				
Repeating words				
Helping other students				
Asking questions				
Discussing stories				
Reading books				
Learning songs				
Doing dictations				
Talking with students				
Talking with my teacher				
Drawing pictures				
Filling in blanks				

Challenge Interview someone about the way he or she learns. Use the ideas in the questionnaire. Write a paragraph about what you learn.

Everyday Conversation

1. Look in your dictionary. Circle the correct answer. What can you say to…?

   a. make sure you understand — "How are things?" / ("Did you say *Tuan*?")

   b. introduce your friend — "Beth, this is Mary." / "Hi, I'm Bud."

   c. apologize — "Excuse me." / "How are you?"

   d. end a conversation — "Good evening." / "Good night."

   e. begin a conversation — "How are you?" / "I'm sorry."

2. Read the start of a romance novel. Match each numbered sentence with its description below.

   ## ～❦ 1 ❦～

   "Ouch!" Nikki cried, as something heavy fell on her foot.

   "I'm really sorry.¹ My science book fell out of my locker," said a deep voice next to her. He picked up the book and stood up. He was tall, and Nikki didn't recognize the handsome face that matched the deep voice.

   "Oh, I'm OK," Nikki said. They walked toward the classrooms.

   "My name's Ben Ives, by the way.² What's yours?"

   "I'm Nikki. Nikki Lewis."³

   Ben stopped and stared. "Did you say *Nikki Lewis*?"⁴ he asked.

   "That's right. Why?" asked Nikki.

   "I heard your piano concert last week. You were great."⁵

   "Thanks."⁶ Now what? Nikki felt her face turning red. She never knew how to begin a conversation.

   "So, how are your classes this year?" Ben asked.

   "They're OK. My English class is fun."

   "Uh-oh, I hear the bell. See you later, Nikki."

   "Nice meeting you, Ben."⁷

   "Hi, Nikki.⁸ Why are you just standing there? Let's get to class!"

   It was Nikki's best friend, Lori.

   ---

   a. _____ Nikki and Ben ended the conversation.

   b. _____ Ben made sure he understood.

   c. _____ Lori greeted Nikki.

   d. _____ Nikki thanked Ben.

   e. _____ Ben introduced himself to Nikki.

   f. _____ Nikki introduced herself to Ben.

   g. __1__ Ben apologized.

   h. _____ Ben complimented Nikki.

Challenge Choose two items from page 8 in your dictionary (for example, beginning and ending a conversation). Make a list of the different ways people do them.

1. Look in your dictionary. What do you need to…?

a. call from a pay phone without coins   _____phone card_____

b. make calls from your car   _____

c. take messages when you're not home   _____

d. walk from room to room when calling someone   _____

e. know if someone is trying to call you   _____

2. Complete this information from a phone book. Use the words in the box.

dial	directory assistance	~~emergency~~	hang up	
international	local	long-distance	operator	pay phone
911	0	phone book	wrong number	

For Fire, Police, or Ambulance 🔥 ⬜ ⚕

• **The number to call in an** _____emergency_____ : _____ .
                                                    a.   **b.**

• **Look it up!** You can avoid calls to _____ by looking up numbers
                                    c.

in the_____ .
        d.

• **Dial direct and save.** Calling another city or state? It costs less when you make a

_____ call yourself. If possible, try not to use the _____ .
    e.   **f.**

• **Ask for credit.** If you reach a _____ , you should _____
                                    g.   **h.**

and _____ "0" immediately. Explain what happened so you can get credit.
      i.

• **Ask for a refund.** If a _____ takes your money but you don't speak to anyone,
                        j.

report it by dialing _____ (operator) from another phone. We'll see that the phone
                      k.

gets repaired and mail you a refund.

To place an _____ call you will need:
                l.

• The country code   • The city code   • The _____ number.
                                                                        m.

Challenge Look at **page 182** in this book. Answer the questions.

Weather

1. Look in your dictionary. Label the weather symbols.

a.  _____sunny_____

d. _____

g. _____

b. _____

e. _____

h. _____

c. _____

f. _____

2. Look at the weather map. Write reports for six cities. Use your own paper.

   Example: *It's windy and very cold in Chicago with temperatures in the 20s.*

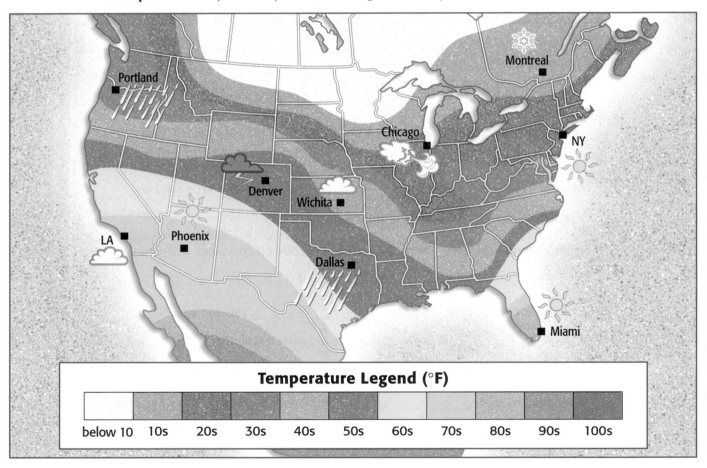

Portland

Montreal

Chicago

NY

Denver

Wichita

LA

Phoenix

Dallas

Miami

Temperature Legend (°F)

below 10	10s	20s	30s	40s	50s	60s	70s	80s	90s	100s

3. What about you? Write today's weather report for your city. Use Exercise 2 as an example.

   _____

   _____

Challenge Look at **page 182** in this book. Follow the instructions.

1. Look in your dictionary. Write all the words that end in *-y*. Then write their opposites.

a. __empty__ __full__   d. _____ _____

b. _____ _____   e. _____ _____

c. _____ _____   f. _____ _____ or _____

2. Look at the classrooms. Find and describe six more differences. Use your own paper.

Example: *Classroom A has a little clock, but the clock in Classroom B is big.*

Classroom A

Classroom B

3. What about you? How does your classroom compare to Classroom A? Write about the differences. Use your own paper.

Challenge Write six sentences that describe this workbook. Use words from page 11 of your dictionary.

Colors

1. Look at **page 65** in your dictionary. What color is the…?

    a. jumpsuit _orange_   **b.** jumper _____   **c.** uniform _____   **d.** tunic _____

2. Look at the article. Circle the correct words to complete the paragraph.

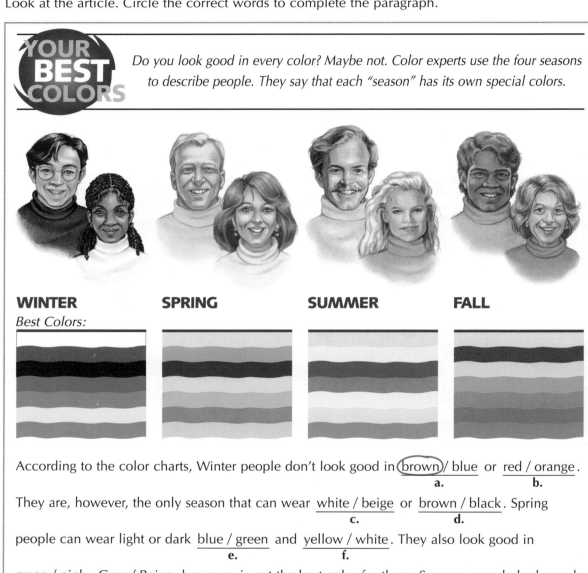

YOUR BEST COLORS

Do you look good in every color? Maybe not. Color experts use the four seasons to describe people. They say that each "season" has its own special colors.

WINTER   **SPRING**   **SUMMER**   **FALL**

Best Colors:

According to the color charts, Winter people don't look good in (brown)/ blue or red / orange .
                                                          a.   **b.**

They are, however, the only season that can wear white / beige or brown / black . Spring
                                             c.   **d.**

people can wear light or dark blue / green and yellow / white . They also look good in
                                       e.   **f.**

green / pink . Gray / Beige , however, is not the best color for them. Summer people look good
 g.   **h.**

in green / gray , but not in orange / yellow . Fall people look great in beige / black , but they
    i.   **j.**   **k.**

can't wear purple / orange . Winter and Fall people can both wear dark brown / turquoise .
         l.   **m.**

And all seasons, except Fall, can wear orange / pink .
                             n.

Challenge Survey your classmates. What colors do they or don't they like to wear?

1. Look at **page 12** in your dictionary. Complete the sentences. Write the locations.

    a. The purple box is _____*above*_____ the pink box.

    b. The gray box is _____ the orange box, on the _____.

    c. The green box is _____ the same shelf as the brown box.

    d. The black box is _____ the white box.

2. Look at the checklist and the picture of the school supply room. Check (✓) the items that are in the correct place.

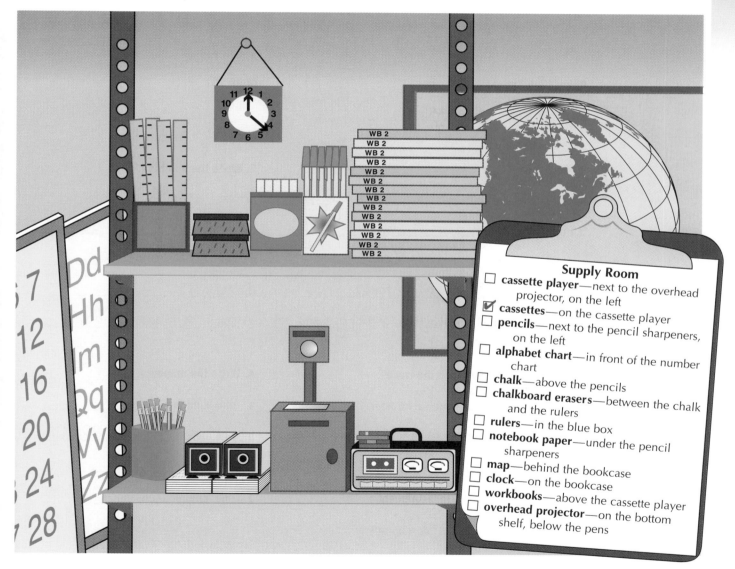

Supply Room

☐ **cassette player**—next to the overhead projector, on the left
☑ **cassettes**—on the cassette player
☐ **pencils**—next to the pencil sharpeners, on the left
☐ **alphabet chart**—in front of the number chart
☐ **chalk**—above the pencils
☐ **chalkboard erasers**—between the chalk and the rulers
☐ **rulers**—in the blue box
☐ **notebook paper**—under the pencil sharpeners
☐ **map**—behind the bookcase
☐ **clock**—on the bookcase
☐ **workbooks**—above the cassette player
☐ **overhead projector**—on the bottom shelf, below the pens

3. Look at Exercise 2. Write about the items that are in the wrong place. Use your own paper.

    Example: *The cassette player is next to the overhead projector, on the right. It isn't on the left.*

Challenge Write a description of your classroom.

Numbers and Measurements

1. Look at the top picture on **pages 2 and 3** in your dictionary.

   a. How many people are male? _____7_____

   b. How many are female? _____

   c. What percent of the people are male? _____

   d. What fraction of the people are female? _____

2. Look at the math test. Circle all the mistakes. Then give the test a percent grade (each question = five points).

Baker High School   **Math 101**

Student's Name: ___Ryan Miller___   _____ %

1. What's next?   **2. Write the numbers.**

a. eleven, twelve, thirteen, ___fourteen___   a. XX ___twenty___

b. one, three, five, ___seven___   b. IX ___nine___

c. two, four, six, ___(ten)___   c. LI ___fifty-one___

d. ten, twenty, thirty, ___forty___   d. IV ___six___

e. ten, one hundred, one thousand, ___ten thousand___   e. CX ___a hundred and ten___

3. Match the numbers with the words.   **4. Write the numbers.**

___1___ a. 12   1. ordinal number   a. one hundred ___100___

___6___ b. DL   2. fraction   b. one million ___1,000,000,000___

___5___ c. 2nd   3. percent   c. ten thousand ___10,000___

___4___ d. 10 in.   4. measurement   d. one hundred thousand ___100,000___

___2___ e. 2/3   5. cardinal number

___3___ f. 98%   6. Roman numeral

---

3. Explain the mistakes on the test in Exercise 2. Use your own paper.

   Example: *Question 1c.—The next number is eight, not ten.*

4. Forty-two percent of the students at Baker High School are female. Which pie chart is correct? Circle the correct letter.

a.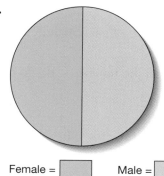

b.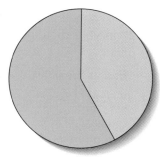

c.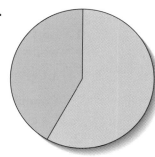

Female = ☐   Male = ☐

5. Students who want to go to college in the United States take the Scholastic Assessment Test (SAT). The highest math score = 800. The lowest math score = 200.

What percent of students scored 400–600 points?

a. forty-seven

b. fifty-three

c. nineteen

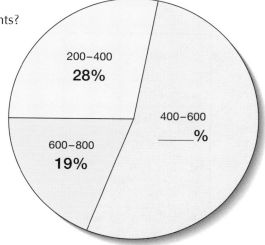

Based on information from the
College Entrance Examination Board, 1993

6. Look at these math SAT scores. Rank the students. (first = the student with the highest score)

NAME	RANK
a. Bob	_____
b. Pam	_____
c. Jan	*first*
d. Lee	_____
e. Mai	_____
f. Bill	_____
g. Ana	_____
h. Todd	_____

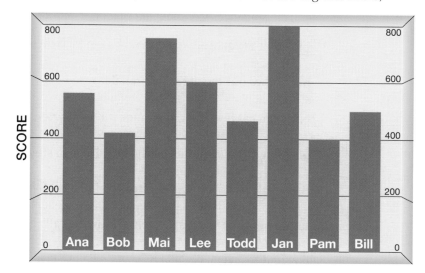

Challenge How many students are in your class? What percent are male? female?
Draw a pie chart like the ones in Exercise 4.

Time

1. Look at **pages 26 and 27** in your dictionary. Write the time of each activity in numbers and words. Use your own paper.

   a. get dressed   **b.** eat breakfast   **c.** clean the house   **d.** go to bed

   Example: *get dressed:*   6:30   six-thirty

2. Look at Nick's time management worksheet. The clocks show the time that he began each activity. Complete his worksheet.

a.  **b.**   **c.**   **d.**   **e.**   **f.**

TIME MANAGEMENT WORKSHEET			
ACTIVITY	TIME BEGAN	TIME ENDED	TOTAL TIME
a. get dressed	7:15 A.M.	8:00 A.M.	45 minutes
b. brush teeth	A.M.	8:01 A.M.	1
c. drive to work		9:00 A.M.	
d. lunch		1:15 P.M.	
e. class		9:15 P.M.	
f. talk to girlfriend		11:40 P.M.	

3. Complete the report. Use the information in Exercise 2.

Before our program, Nick was taking forty-five seconds /(minutes) to get dressed, from a quarter
a.
to / after seven until eight P.M. / o'clock. Now it takes him fifteen hours / minutes (he puts
b. **c.** **d.**
his clothes out the night before). Because he finishes getting dressed by seven -thirty / -fifteen,
e.
Nick can eat breakfast, brush for three minutes, and catch an eight hour / o'clock bus instead
f.
of driving. Nick studies on the bus. He also studies for the first forty minutes of his lunch hour,

from half past / a quarter after twelve until five to / after one. Nick used to talk to his girlfriend
g. **h.**
until twenty to eleven / twelve. Now he calls her forty minutes earlier, at twenty to / half past
i. **j.**
ten, and he gets more sleep.

4. What about you? How long does it take you to do everyday activities? Write five sentences.

16

5. Look at the time-zone map in your dictionary. Complete these notes.

a.
Flight 20 Q ✈
flying time: 6 hours
leave NY 10:30 a.m. (eastern time)
arrive LA _1:30 p.m._ (Pacific time)

c.
Flight 34 Q ✈
flying time: 3 1/2 hours
leave Chicago 12:00 p.m. (central time)
arrive Halifax _____ (Atlantic time)

b.
Flight 453 Q ✈
flying time: 7 hours
leave Phoenix 8:00 p.m. (mountain time)
arrive Anchorage _____ (Alaska time)

d.
Flight 733 Q ✈
flying time: 4 hours
leave Detroit 8:00 a.m. (eastern time)
arrive Dallas _____ (central time)

6. Complete the article. Use the words in the box. (You will use two words more than once.) Use your dictionary for help.

| Atlantic | daylight saving | earlier | later | Pacific | standard | time zones |

It's a Question of Time

In 1884, people in different countries agreed to have _standard_ time. They
a.
divided the world into 24 _____. Some large countries have more than one. The
b.
continental United States, for example, has four. These are eastern, central, mountain, and

_____. Alaska and Hawaii have their own time zones. Canada has two others.
c.
These are Newfoundland and _____ time.
d.
The time difference between one zone and the next is one hour. For example, when it's noon

eastern time, it's 1:00 P.M. _____ time. (That's one hour _____.)
e. **f.**
At the same time, it's 11:00 A.M. central time. (That's one hour _____.)
g.
Many countries change the clock in order to use more hours of light in the summer. This

is called _____ time. In the United States, it begins the first Sunday in April and
h.
ends the last Sunday in October. The country then returns to _____ time.
i.

Challenge Look at **page 182** in this book. Follow the instructions.

1. Look at **page 19** in your dictionary. Compare June to December 2001. Which month…?

a. has more days _____

b. begins on a weekday _____

2. Read Eva's e-mail. Then complete her calendar for April.

Subj: your visit
Date: 4-10-99 12:07:11 EST
From: EvaL@uol.com

Hi Dania! It's Saturday night. I just returned to Miami yesterday. There were no classes for a week so I flew to Chicago last Saturday to visit my parents. Classes begin again on Monday. It's a busy semester. I have English three times a week (Mondays, Wednesdays, and Fridays). I usually have language lab every Thursday, too. Next week, however, there's no language lab—I go to computer lab instead. In addition to English, I'm studying science. Science meets twice a week on the days that I don't have English. And there's science lab on Tuesdays.

Last Sunday, daylight saving time began. Do you have that in Canada? I like it a lot. The days seem much longer.

I'm glad it's the weekend. Tomorrow I'm seeing Tom. (I told you about him in my last letter.) I've got to go now. On Saturdays I go to the gym to work out. We can go together when you come! I'm really looking forward to your visit. Just two weeks from today!

Eva
P.S. Bring your appetite! On Sunday there's a cake sale at the school cafeteria.

1999			*April*			1999
S	**M**	**T**	**W**	**T**	**F**	**S**
				1	2	3
4	5	6	7	8	9 *Return to Miami*	10
11	12	13	14	15	16	17
18	19	20	21	22	23	24
25	26	27	28	29	30	

3. What about you? Write a letter to a friend. Describe your weekly schedule. Use your own paper.

4. Look in your dictionary. Write the season.

   a. Tim's birthday _____ spring _____

   b. Easter _____

   c. the man and woman's anniversary _____

   d. the man's vacation _____

5. Read the information. Write the season next to each holiday.

Legal Holidays—U.S. 2006

a. _____ winter _____	Christmas	12/25	
b. _____	Columbus Day	10/9	*(2nd Mon. of the month)*
c. _____	Independence Day	7/4	
d. _____	Labor Day	9/4	*(1st Mon. of the month)*
e. _____	Martin Luther King Jr.'s Birthday	1/16	*(3rd Mon. of the month)*
f. _____	Memorial Day	5/29	*(last Mon. of the month)*
g. _____	New Year's Day	1/1	
h. _____	Thanksgiving Day	11/23	*(4th Thurs. of the month)*
i. _____	Veterans Day	11/11	
j. _____	President's Day	2/20	*(3rd Mon. of the month)*

6. Look at the chart in Exercise 5. Put the holidays in the correct time order in the columns below. Write the seasons and the months in words.

   _____ Winter _____

   Date   Holiday

   January 1   New Year's Day

Date   Holiday

Date   Holiday

Date   Holiday

7. Look at the chart in Exercise 5. Which months do not have any legal holidays?

_____ March _____ , _____ , _____ , _____

Challenge Look at the chart on **page 182** in this book. Follow the instructions.

Money

1. Look in your dictionary. On your own paper, write the fewest coins and bills you can use to make….

   a. $7.05 **b.** $.64 **c.** $1.37 **d.** $380

   Example: *$7.05: a five-dollar bill, two one-dollar bills, and…*

2. Look at the chart. Then complete the statements below. Use words, not numbers.

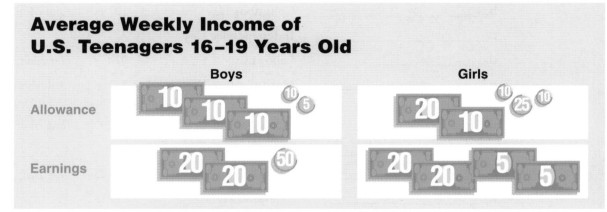

Average Weekly Income of U.S. Teenagers 16–19 Years Old

Based on information from the Rand Youth Poll, New York City (1993 information)

   a. A boy's allowance is ___thirty dollars and fifteen cents___.

   b. A girl's allowance is _____ more than a boy's.

   c. A boy earns _____.

   d. Girls earn _____ more than boys earn.

   e. A teenage girl earns _____.

3. Read the statements and write the method of payment.

How do today's teens pay for things?

   a. It's great for clothes shopping, but my parents had to sign the application.
   —Mona Damon, Valley High School
   ___credit card___

   b. Every time I write one, I record the date and the amount, so I know how much I'm spending every month.
   —Mikio Sato, Taylor University
   _____

   c. I don't have a credit card or a checking account yet, so I use these. I have to go to the post office to buy them.
   —Amanda Davis, Danton Middle School
   _____

   d. I'll use them on my trip to Mexico during my junior year.
   —Paul Riley, Short Hills High School
   _____

Challenge Write at least ten combinations of bills and coins that equal $2.10.

1. Look in your dictionary. Another customer bought sweaters at the same sale. Read the conversation and complete the receipt.

Customer: I'll take the blue and the green.

Clerk: Cash or credit card?

Customer: Cash. Do you have change for $100?

Clerk: Certainly.

```
        Clothesmart
          4•15•01
  2
 ____ sweater
@ _____
                        _____
 _____ @ ____ %      1.65
 Amount due
 Amount tendered         _____

                         _____
                          78.37
```

2. Circle the correct words to complete the shopper's advice column.

Q Recently, I bought a microwave at the (regular) sale price. A week later, I saw it at the
　　　　　　　　　　　　　　　　　a.

same store for 20% less. Is there anything I can do?

A Some stores will give you the cheaper price if you show your sales tax / receipt . That's
　　　　　　　　　　　　　　　　　　　　　　　　　　　　　　　　b.

why you should always keep / sell it.
　　　　　　　　　　　　　c.

Q I gave my nephew a sweater for his birthday. He wants to exchange / return it and use
　　　　　　　　　　　　　　　　　　　　　　　　　　　　　d.

the money for a music CD. When I paid for / sold it, it was $19.99. Now the store is
　　　　　　　　　　　　　　　　e.

having a big sale, and it's only $9.99. How much will they give him?

A Give him the receipt / change and total / price tag to show the store. He should
　　　　　　　　　　f.　　　　　　**g.**

get $19.99.

Q I bought three pairs of jeans. The sales tax / price tag showed $14.99 each, but the
　　　　　　　　　　　　　　　　　　　　h.

cash register showed only $26.97. The clerk said the jeans just went on sale. How did

the cash register know?

A The new price / tax was in the store computer. When the computer "read" the
　　　　　　i.

receipt / bar code (those black lines), the cash register showed the correct change / total .
　　j.　　　　　　　　　　　　　　　　　　　　　　　　　　　　　　**k.**

What a nice surprise!

Challenge Write a question for the shopper's advice column.

▶ **Go to page 170 for Another Look (Unit 1).**

Age and Physical Description

1. Look in your dictionary. Complete the chart. Use the words in the box.

Height
~~Man~~
Age
Woman
Weight

Mr. and Ms. Average American		
	Man	
_____	33 years old	35 years old
_____	170 lbs. (76.5kg)	140 lbs. (63kg)
_____	5'10" (1.75m)	5'4" (1.60m)

Based on information from combined U.S. Government Statistics

2. Circle the correct words to complete the article.

An Average Supermodel

22 years old
6 feet
125 pounds

Sheri Snow is an average model, but she is NOT an average American woman. To begin with, she's middle-aged / (young): only 22 years old.
a.
The average age for women in the U.S. is 35. And at 6 feet, Sheri is also

not average height / tall. Like most models, she is tall / short and quite
b. **c.**
thin / heavyset. (Her weight / age stays at about 125 pounds.) However, the
d. **e.**
most obvious difference may be her looks. The average American woman

is good-looking, but she can't compare to this very, very attractive supermodel.

Those good looks got Sheri her first job early—as a cute / middle-aged, two-year-old baby / toddler in
f. **g.**
TV commercials. Then, when she was a ten-year-old senior citizen / girl, she entered a *Pre-Teen Magazine*
h.
contest. Sheri won the contest, and hasn't stopped since. At 20, she met her husband. While she was

pregnant / physically challenged, Sheri modeled clothes for mothers-to-be. Now the couple has a
i.
three-year-old / three-month-old baby. Sheri has no plans to quit. "When I'm 75, I plan to model clothes
j.
for elderly women / teenagers," she says.
k.

_____ **Challenge** Compare yourself or someone you know to the average American man or woman.

1. Look at the women at the bottom of your dictionary page. Who said…?

   a. "I use bigger rollers at home."   *the woman in picture C*

   b. "Wow! Great color!"   _____

   c. "Please cut it very short."   _____

   d. "Will this perm take a long time?"   _____

2. Complete the advice column with the words in the box.

perm	color	cut	long	mustache	~~gray~~	wavy	beard	blow dryer

HAIRY PROBLEMS

Q I'm only twenty, but I've got a lot of _____*gray*_____ hair.
                            a.

A Why not _____ it? Ask your hairdresser about the shade.
             b.

Q My boyfriend loves _____ hair, but I want short hair this summer.
                       c.

A _____ it a little at a time. Stop when you both like the length.
        d.

Q I want _____ hair, but I hate rollers.
                e.

A _____ it. You'll have the style you want with no work.
      f.

Q I always use a _____ after I shampoo. Is hot air bad for my hair?
                 g.

A Yes. Use a towel some of the time.

Q My husband says he spends too much time shaving.

A Tell him to grow a _____ and a _____. He'll have to shave less!
                  h.   **i.**

3. Find and correct four more mistakes in this advertisement.

Mom has beautiful, shoulder-length, ~~curly~~ *straight* blond hair. Dad has long, curly black hair. Erica has shoulder-length, wavy brown hair. They all have great haircuts from Kindest Cuts. **_Still only $15._**

Challenge Look in a magazine, newspaper, or your picture dictionary. Find a hairstyle you like. Describe what a stylist did to create the style.

Family

1. Look at page 24 in your dictionary. Who said…?
   a. "I play softball with my two brothers."   _____Lily_____
   b. "My baby brother just started to walk."   _____
   c. "I don't have any brothers or sisters."   _____
   d. "Aunt Ana made a pretty dress for me."   _____

2. Complete the family tree. Show the people's relationship to Diana.

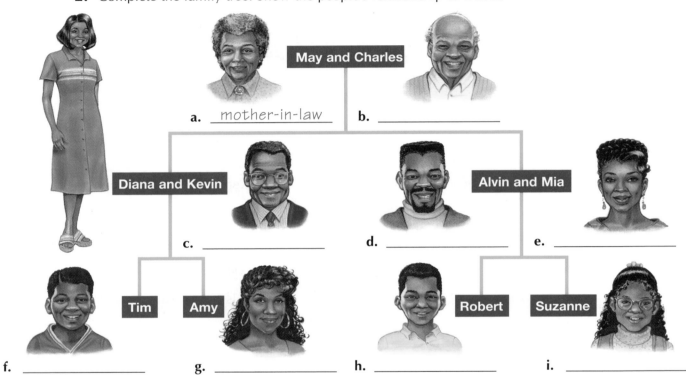

May and Charles

a. _mother-in-law_   b. _____

Diana and Kevin

Alvin and Mia

c. _____   d. _____   e. _____

Tim   **Amy**   **Robert**   **Suzanne**

f. _____   g. _____   h. _____   i. _____

3. Look at Diana's niece Suzanne in Exercise 2. Use information from the family tree to complete this paragraph from Suzanne's letter.

This week my _____cousin_____ Amy turned sixteen, so my _____
                  a.   b.
Kevin and my _____ Diana gave her a big party. My _____
              c.   d.
Robert and I played with the younger children, and my _____were very
                                                       e.
busy too – Mom helped serve the food, and Dad took lots of pictures of Amy,
their only _____. In the middle of the party someone shouted, "May
            f.
is on the telephone." It was our _____ calling from San Francisco!
                                  g.

4. What about you? Draw your family tree. Use your own paper.

24

5. Look at page 25 in your dictionary. **True** or **False**?

a. David's father is Lisa's stepfather. _____True_____

b. Kim's mother is married to Lisa's father. _____

c. Mary and Kim are stepsisters. _____

d. Carol is divorced from Bill's stepfather. _____

6. Complete the entries from Lisa's diary. Use the words in the box. (You will use two words more than once.)

divorced	**half sister**	**married**	**remarried**
single father	**stepfather**	**stepmother**	

3/15/96-Dad moved away this week. He and Mom got___divorced___.
_____**a.**
That means they're not _____ anymore. I feel bad, but
_____**b.**
Mom says I didn't do anything wrong.

4/1/96-Dad's new apartment is cool. He says he'll always be my
father, but now he's a _____, not a married one.
_____**c.**

10/4/98-Mom says she wants to get _____ someday. That
_____**d.**
man Rick seems nice.

12/10/98-Mom and Rick got _____! Rick's my _____
_____**e.**_____**f.**
now. I wonder—can I still visit Dad?

12/12/98-I had a great time at Dad's this weekend. We went to the
circus with Bill and Kim. When Dad and Sue get married, he'll be
Bill and Kim's _____, and Sue will be my _____.
_____**g.**_____**h.**

11/14/99-We have a new baby! Her name is Mary. I'm her
_____. Mom says I can help take care of her.
_____**i.**

Challenge Look at **page 183** in this book. Follow the instructions.

Daily Routines

1. Look in your dictionary. Complete the schedule.

TIME	Mai	David
6:00 A.M.	get up	wake up
6:30 A.M.	take a shower	get dressed
7:00 A.M.	make lunch	
8:00 A.M.		drive to work
10:00 A.M.	school	
6:00 P.M.	cook dinner	
6:30 P.M.		have dinner
10:30 P.M.		go to bed

2. Read this article about the family in your dictionary. Find and <u>underline</u> five more mistakes. Use your dictionary for help.

The Fast Track Family

David and Mai Lim want a lot from life, and their daily routine shows it. In the morning, David gets up <u>before</u> Mai. Mai takes a shower while David gets dressed. Then David eats breakfast with the kids and Mai makes lunch. At 7:30, Mai takes the kids to school. Mai, a full-time student, is in school all day. David stays home. Between 4:30 and 6:00, Mai goes to the market, cleans the house, and cooks dinner. During that time, David leaves work and picks up the kids at daycare. The family eats dinner together. Then Mai does homework, and David reads the paper. They go to sleep at 10:30. It's a busy schedule, but the Lims enjoy it. ■

3. Explain the mistakes in Exercise 2.

a. <u>David doesn't get up before Mai. He gets up after her.</u>

b. _____

c. _____

d. _____

e. _____

f. _____

4. Make questions from the scrambled words.

a. time   What   you   up   do   get

<u>What time do you get up?</u>

b. eat   breakfast   When   you   do

_____

c. you   leave   When   the   house   do

_____

d. home   come   you   do   time   What

_____

e. to   bed   go   do   When   you

_____

5. What about you? Complete the chart with information about your daily routine. Then interview another person. Use questions like the ones in Exercise 4.

Your name: _____		Your partner's name: _____	
ACTIVITY	**TIME**	**ACTIVITY**	**TIME**

Challenge Compare the routines in Exercise 5. Write six sentences. Use _after_, _before_, or _while_ in some of your sentences. **Example:** _I get up before Kyung, but we both leave for class at 8:00._

Life Events

1. Look in your dictionary. How old was Martin Perez when he…?

   a. started school   _5_   **e.** had his first child   _____

   b. joined the army   _____   **f.** bought his first house   _____

   c. became a citizen   _____   **g.** had his first grandchild   _____

   d. got married   _____   **h.** died   _____

2. Complete this biography about photographer Alfred Eisenstaedt. Use the past tense form of the words in the boxes.

EISENSTAEDT, ALFRED (1898–1995)

| ~~be born~~ | move | rent |

Alfred Eisenstaedt was one of the greatest photographers in

the world. He ___was born___ in Dirschau, Germany, in 1898.
     a.

When he was eight, his family _____ to Berlin.
                        b.

There they _____ a large, comfortable apartment. He got his first camera
           c.

at the age of 14, but he was not very interested in it.

| get | go | join |

Alfred _____ the army in 1916. After the army, he returned to Berlin
          d.

and _____ to college. Times were difficult, and soon he left college and
     e.

_____ a job selling clothes.
   f.

| become | get | travel |

When he was 24, Eisenstaedt saved money and _____ his first
                                    g.

Leica (a small, fast camera). Five years later, he _____ a professional
                                   h.

photographer. He _____ to France, Switzerland, Italy, and Ethiopia taking
               i.

pictures. People were his favorite subject.

```
die        get married        immigrate        join
```

In 1935, Eisenstaedt _____ to the United States. A year later, he
                              j.

_____ the staff of *Life* magazine. He worked there 36 years. After he
         k.

stopped working, he and his wife Alma (the two _____ in 1949) lived on
                                                         l.

Martha's Vineyard. He _____ there in 1995, at the age of 96.
                              m.

3. Read the statements about Alfred Eisenstaedt. **True** or **False**? Write a question mark (**?**) if the information isn't in the reading in Exercise 2.

    a. Alfred Eisenstaedt was born in the United States.   <u> False </u>

    b. He moved to Berlin in 1906.   <u>   </u>

    c. He became a citizen of the United States.   <u>   </u>

    d. Eisenstaedt got married before he immigrated to the U.S.   <u>   </u>

    e. His wife had a baby in 1951.   <u>   </u>

    f. He lived in the United States for 60 years.   <u>   </u>

4. Check (✔) the documents Alfred Eisenstaedt probably had. Use the information in Exercise 2.

    ☐ high school diploma   ☐ college degree   ☐ marriage license   ☐ passport

5. Complete the time line for Alfred Eisenstaedt. Use the information in Exercise 2.

EVENT	was born	moved to Berlin		joined the army	became a photographer		
YEAR	1898	1912		1935	1936	1949	1995

6. What about you? Draw a time line with your own information. Then, write a short autobiography. Use your own paper.

Challenge Think of a famous person and look up biographical information about him or her. Draw a time line and write a paragraph about the person's life.

Feelings

1. Look in your dictionary. Find and write the opposite of these words.

a. comfortable   <u>uncomfortable</u>   d. sick   _____

b. hot   _____   e. happy   _____

c. nervous   _____   f. full   _____

2. Read the conversations. Complete each sentence with a word from the box.

Ana: What's the matter?

Hisae: I really miss my family.

Hisae feels ____<u>homesick</u>____ .
           a.

hurt	~~homesick~~	sick

Alfons: Ow!

Carla: What's wrong?

Alfons: It's my heart!

Alfons is _____ .
         b.

homesick	in love	in pain

Tom: I can't eat *that!*

Julia: Why not?

Tom: It looks and smells just terrible!

Tom is _____ .
       c.

disgusted	sick	nervous

Laurel: There you are! It's almost 10:30!

Andy: Sorry. The train was late.

Laurel: I'm glad you're OK. I was worried.

Laurel is _____ .
          d.

angry	confused	relieved

Jennifer: Would you like some more?

Bill: Oh, no thanks. I can't have another bite!

Bill feels _____ .
           e.

full	hungry	thirsty

3. Circle the correct words to complete the story.

Min Hau had so many feelings his first day of school. When he left home, he felt

(scared) / excited. His mother looked nervous / calm, but his little brother just looked
   a.   **b.**

sad / sleepy. When he got to school, he walked into the wrong class. The teacher looked
   c.

bored / surprised, and Min Hau was very embarrassed / worried. He felt much better in math
   d.   **e.**

class. He was proud / shocked when he did a problem correctly. His teacher looked
           f.

happy / surprised. At lunchtime, he looked at his food and felt confused / disgusted.
   g.   **h.**

"What is this?" As he sat in the cafeteria, Min Hau was feeling awfully tired / lonely. Then
                                                    i.

someone said, "Can I sit here?" Suddenly his feelings changed. Was he in love / in pain?
                                                               j.

4. What about you? How did you feel on your first day of school? Write sentences on your own paper.

Challenge Look at **page 183** in this book. Follow the instructions.

1. Look in your dictionary. Who said…?

a. "I'm happy to be here today. I remember my own graduation." ___guest speaker___

b. "Please, everyone, look over here. Now, smile!" _____

c. "My four years here have been wonderful." _____

2. Complete the article. Use the words in the box.

applauded	audience	class	cried	diplomas
gowns	guest speaker	graduated	graduates	~~podium~~
speech	stage	took	valedictorian	

Mayor Attends Graduation

Mayor Rodriguez behind the
___podium___ .
a.

GREENVILLE, JUNE 11—Yesterday was Bryant College's fiftieth graduation ceremony. The event took place in the school's large auditorium. This year's graduating _____ had 78 _____ .
      b.   **c.**

In their purple caps and _____ , they
           d.

walked proudly across the large _____
           e.

to receive their _____ .
      f.

The _____ , graduating senior, Cathy
     g.

Chan, gave a beautiful _____ .
           h.

The _____ of proud friends and
      i.

family _____ loudly at the end.
    j.

Mrs. Chan _____ tears of happiness.
      k.

This year's _____ was Greenville's
       l.

own mayor, Lillian Rodriguez. Mayor Rodriguez herself

_____ from Bryant in 1970. Rodriguez
     m.

spoke about jobs, schools, and family as the photographer

_____ pictures.
   n.

3. Look in your dictionary. Who said…?

    a. "Can I give you some more chicken? Something to drink?"   _caterer_

    b. "And next, we're going to hear a song called 'School's Out.'"   _____

    c. "This is a great party. Thanks for inviting us!"   _____

4. Look at the pictures. Find and describe eight more differences. Use your own paper.

    Example: _There are ten guests on Ana's dance floor. There are eight guests on Brian's dance floor._

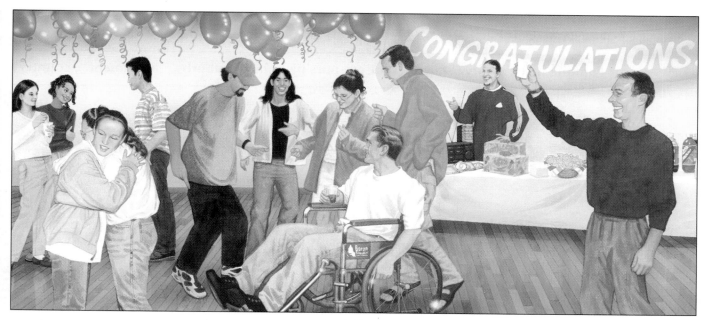

Ana's Party

Brian's Party

Challenge   Write a newspaper report of a graduation you have attended or the one in your dictionary.

▶ **Go to page 171 for Another Look (Unit 2).**

Places to Live

1. Look in your dictionary. Where can you hear…?

a. "My roommate is studying chemistry."   college dormitory

b. "I became homeless after I lost my job."   _____

c. "We raise horses."   _____

d. "All four houses look the same."   _____

2. Complete the letter. Use the words in the box.

mobile home   city   ~~farm~~   house   nursing home   suburbs   apartment   country

Dear Fran,

    You asked me to tell you about the places I have lived. I hope I can remember them all. I grew up on a potato _____farm_____ in Ireland. Not long after your grandfather and I got
            a.
married, we immigrated to America. For five years, we rented a little _____ in
                                                                b.
an old building. I didn't like living in a big _____ like Boston. I really prefer
                                         c.
living in the _____, where I grew up. I was happy when we bought our own
                  d.
_____ in the _____, only 15 miles from the city. It had a yard,
  e.   **f.**
and your father had his own bedroom. We lived there for 20 years. When your grandfather stopped working, we wanted to travel. We bought a _____, and for a while, we
                                                          g.
moved our little home every few years! After your grandfather died, I couldn't get around very well or live alone anymore, so I moved here. When you were little, you used to think that all the elderly people here in the _____ were your grandparents, too. We're
                                                       h.
all looking forward to your next visit.

                                        Love,
                                        Grandma

3. What about you? Americans move an average of 30 times in their lives. Where have you lived? Make a chart like the one below. Use your own paper.

PLACE NAME	CITY, SUBURBS, OR COUNTRY	TYPE OF HOME	YEAR YOU MOVED THERE	HOW LONG YOU LIVED THERE
New York	city	apartment	1998	3 years

Challenge Write a paragraph about the places you've lived. Use information from Exercise 3.

34

1. Look in your dictionary. What are they doing?

a. "How about $125,000?" _____making an offer_____

b. "Let's put the table there, in front of the love seat." _____

c. "The keys to our new house! Thank you." _____

d. "Thank you. Now we have the money for the house!" _____

2. Circle the correct words to complete the article.

Home Improvement

The rent is too high and the rooms are too small, but this time you're not going to just (look for) / get a loan for a bigger **a.** apartment. And you're not going to sign a lease / arrange the **b.** furniture and continue to pay rent every month. You're going to make the big move and rent an apartment / buy a house! **c.** You're excited but nervous. Here are some suggestions that will make things easier.

First, make a checklist. Are schools important? Shopping? Write it all down. Next, talk to a Realtor / manager. Explain **d.** how much you can pay and go over your checklist. With that information, he or she can take ownership of / look for houses **e.**

that match your needs. Be patient. Most buyers look at seven to twelve homes before they decide.

When you find your dream house, make an offer / move in **f.** quickly, or you might lose it to another buyer. If you and the sellers agree on the price, it's time to unpack / get a loan. **g.** This can take a long time. Again, be patient.

Finally the happy day comes. The seller hands you the keys and you sign a rental agreement / take ownership! Now **h.** all you have to do is move in, unpack / sign a lease, and **i.** arrange the furniture. Oh, and pay the rent / mortgage, **j.** of course.

3. What about you? Check (✓) all the items that are important to you.

• R E A L T Y •

TYPE	☐ APARTMENT	☐ HOUSE	☐ OTHER:_____
LOCATION	☐ CITY	☐ SUBURBS	☐ COUNTRY
NEAR	☐ SCHOOLS	☐ SHOPPING	☐ WORK
SPACE	☐ NUMBER OF ROOMS	☐ SIZE OF ROOMS	
COST	☐ RENT	☐ MORTGAGE	

Challenge Write a paragraph about a time you looked for and found a new home.

Apartments

1. Look in your dictionary. Where can you hear...?

   a. "We're going up now."   <u>in the elevator</u>

   b. "Come in. The water's great!"   _____

   c. "All I ever get are bills and ads."   _____

   d. "It's beautiful up here. What a great view!"   _____

   e. "Someone's car is in my space."   _____

   f. "Your things will be dry in five minutes."   _____

2. Circle the correct words to complete this ad.

The Glenwood Manor

1- and 2-Bedroom apartments now available!

We just hung out a fire escape /(vacancy sign!)
a.

> **Enjoy suburban living in the middle of the city!**
> **The Glenwood has it all...**

Security
- 24-hour <u>doorman / landlord</u>
  b.
- <u>Intercom / Trash chute</u> in every apartment
  c.

Comfort
- All apartments come with <u>trash bins / air conditioners</u>
  d.
- Some apartments available with <u>balconies / entrances</u>
  e.
- Beautiful <u>roof garden / security gate</u>
  f.

Convenience
- 20-car <u>courtyard / garage</u> (Every apartment has its own free <u>fire exit / parking space.</u>)
  g.   h.
- <u>Laundry room / Swimming pool</u> on every floor (All new washers and dryers.)
  i.
- <u>Elevator / Playground</u> for children
  j.
- <u>Alley / Rec room</u> with exercise equipment
  k.

For more information, contact our <u>manager / tenant</u>: John Miller 555-4334
l.

3. Complete this pamphlet. Use the words in the box.

dead-bolt	door chain	doorknob	elevator	fire escape
intercom	~~neighbors~~	peephole	smoke detector	stairs

BETTER SAFE THAN SORRY!

■ Know your ___neighbors___.
  a.
Don't allow strangers into the
building.

■ Always use your _____
  b.
to ask "Who's there?"

■ Look out your _____
  c.
before you open your apartment
door.

■ When you're at home, keep
your _____ on.
  d.

■ Install a _____.
  e.
It's the strongest lock.

■ Keep a _____
  f.
on the wall or ceiling between your
bedroom and your apartment door.
Check it every month!

■ In case of fire, do not use the
_____. (The heat
  g.
can cause it to stop between
floors.) Use the _____
  h.
instead.

■ Feel the _____ of your
  i.
apartment. If it's hot, the fire may be
out in the hall. Use the _____
  j.
_____ to leave your apartment.

For serious emergencies dial 911.
All other times call your local
police or fire department.

4. What about you? How safe is your home? Check (✓) the things your home has.

☐ smoke detector   ☐ fire escape   ☐ fire exit   ☐ intercom

☐ security system   ☐ security gate   ☐ dead-bolt lock   ☐ peephole

☐ door chain   ☐ Other: _____

Challenge Describe the ideal apartment building.

1. Look at the house in your dictionary. Choose the correct ad for it.

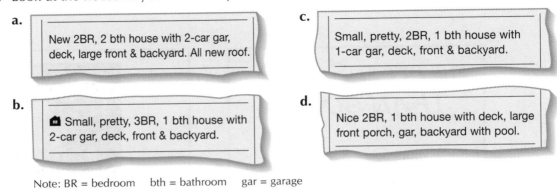

a.

> New 2BR, 2 bth house with 2-car gar, deck, large front & backyard. All new roof.

c.

> Small, pretty, 2BR, 1 bth house with 1-car gar, deck, front & backyard.

b.

> 🏠 Small, pretty, 3BR, 1 bth house with 2-car gar, deck, front & backyard.

d.

> Nice 2BR, 1 bth house with deck, large front porch, gar, backyard with pool.

Note: BR = bedroom   bth = bathroom   gar = garage

2. Look at the houses. Find and describe 11 more differences. Use your own paper.

Example: *10 Pine Street's chimney is on the right, but 12's is on the left.*

10 Pine Street   **12 Pine Street**

_____ **Challenge** Find an apartment ad in the newspaper. Describe the apartment.

1. Look in your dictionary. What can you use to…?

   a. cook outdoors   _barbecue grill_

   b. clean leaves from the lawn   or

   c. lie down and read

   d. carry compost

   e. water the lawn

   f. cut branches from bushes

   g. water the flowers near the patio

   h. plant a tree

2. Circle the correct words to complete the article. Look at **pages 132–134** in your dictionary for help.

e're planning to change our yard into a wildlife habitat—a home for birds and animals.

Next to our patio, we're going to plant (bushes) / flowerpots where rabbits and squirrels can hide.
                                                       a.

We want two big trowels / trees that will be homes for squirrels and bats, and a thick hedge / hose
                      b.   **c.**
in the back where rabbits and other small animals can live. To attract butterflies, we'll plant colorful

compost / flowers at the edge of the patio. The patio furniture / lawn will be very small because
        d.   **e.**
animals don't like open spaces—that means we'll have less to mow!

3. What about you? Plan your ideal yard. Check (✔) the items you would like.

   ☐ trees   ☐ a hammock   ☐ flowers   ☐ a compost pile

   ☐ a lawn   ☐ bushes   ☐ hedges   ☐ a patio

   ☐ a barbecue grill   ☐ Other: _____

Challenge Draw your ideal yard and write a paragraph describing it.

A Kitchen

1. Look in your dictionary. What is <u>it</u>?

    a. <u>It</u>'s on the right back burner of the stove.   _teakettle_

    b. <u>It</u>'s on the counter, to the left of the sink.   _____

    c. <u>They</u>'re on the wall, under the cabinets.   _____

    d. <u>It</u>'s below the oven.   _____

2. Look at the chart. **True** or **False**?

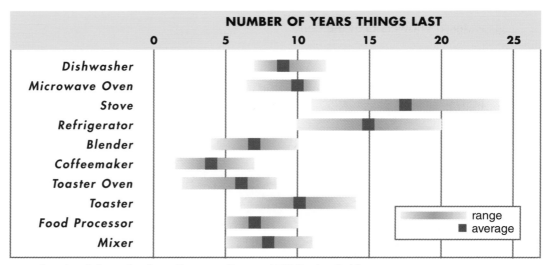

Based on information from _Consumer Reports 1997 Buying Guide_

    a. A ![coffeemaker] lasts an average of ten years.   _False_

    b. A ![dishwasher] lasts an average of about nine years.   _____

    c. A lasts longer than a .   _____

    d. The average life of a ![toaster oven] is shorter than the life of a .   _____

    e. A ![refrigerator] lasts from about ten to twenty years.   _____

    f. A ![stove] doesn't last as long as a .   _____

3. What about you? List the kitchen appliances from Exercise 2 that you have. Use your own paper. How long have you had them? **Example:** _mixer—2 years_

Challenge   Which five kitchen appliances are the most important? Why?

1. Look in your dictionary. List the items on the table. Use your own paper.

Example: *5 place mats*

2. Complete the conversations. Use the words in the box.

candles	ceiling fan	creamer	serving dish	~~tablecloth~~	tray	vase

a. Alek: I'm setting the table. Are we going to use place mats?

    Ella: No. Put on the white _____tablecloth_____ instead.

b. Alek: Is it hot in here?

    Ella: Yes. Why don't you turn on the _____?

c. Alek: What beautiful flowers!

    Ella: I'll get a _____ for them.

d. Alek: Are we going to serve each guest a piece of fish?

    Ella: No. I'm going to put the fish on a _____ in the middle of the table. That way people can take as much as they want.

e. Alek: Where should I put the coffee cups?

    Ella: I'll carry them out on a _____ after we finish eating.

f. Alek: Could you pour some milk in the _____ and bring it out with the sugar bowl?

    Ella: Sure.

g. Alek: It was a lovely dinner party.

    Ella: Yes, it was. Can I blow out the _____ now?

3. What about you? Draw a picture of the table at a dinner you had. Label the items. Use your own paper.

Challenge Find a picture of a dining area in a newspaper or magazine. Describe it.

1. Look in your dictionary. **True** or **False**? Correct the underlined words in the false sentences.

       stereo system

    a. There's a ~~TV~~ in the wall unit.   _____*False*_____

    b. There's a <u>fire</u> in the fireplace.   _____

    c. There's a painting over the <u>mantle</u>.   _____

    d. The magazine holder is next to the <u>fire screen</u>.   _____

    e. There are throw pillows on the <u>armchair</u>.   _____

2. Look at the pictures. Circle the correct words to complete the sentences.

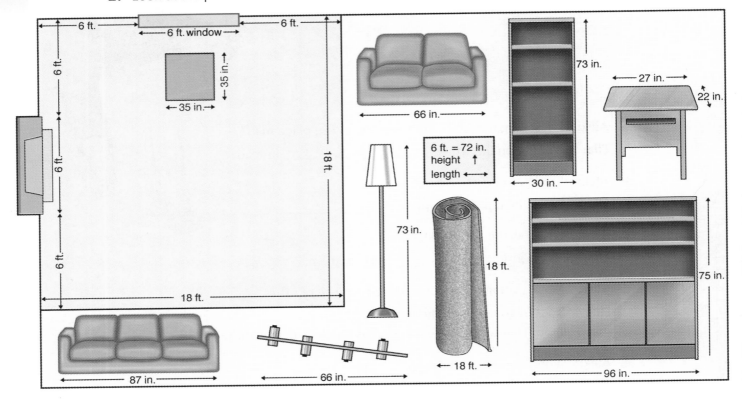

    a. The (coffee table) / end table is already in the living room.

    b. The bookcase / wall unit can go to the left of the window.

    c. The sofa / love seat fits to the right of the window.

    d. The track lighting is the same length as the love seat / fireplace.

    e. The carpet is bigger than / the same size as the living room.

    f. The floor lamp is the same height as the bookcase / wall unit.

3. What about you? Draw a floor plan of your living room. Label the items. Use your own paper.

Challenge   How would you decorate the living room in Exercise 2? Write sentences. **Example:** *I'd put the sofa in the middle of the living room, across from the window…*

1. Look in your dictionary. Which item is each person talking about?

a. "Can I put my dirty jeans in <u>here</u>?"   _hamper_

b. "Look at <u>that</u>! You weigh 55 pounds!"   _____

c. "I just used the <u>last roll</u>. Do we have any more?"   _____

d. "I'm going to hang your towel and washcloth <u>here</u>." _____

e. "There's hair in <u>it</u>. The water's not going down."   _____

f. "Let's open <u>these</u> so we have more light."   _____

2. Complete the article. Use the words in the box.

sink	hot water	medicine cabinet	soap dish	showerhead
rubber mat	toilet	bath mat	wastebasket	~~bathtub~~ faucets

Keep bath time safe and happy by following these safety rules:

1. Never leave a young child alone in the ___ _bathtub_ ___ . Even small amounts of water can
              a.
be dangerous.

2. Avoid burns from _____ . Turn the temperature on your water heater down
         b.
to 100°F. Fix any dripping _____ , and don't forget the _____ —hot
            c.   **d.**
drops from above can hurt too.

3. Prevent falls. Keep a _____ in the bathtub or stall shower
           e.
and a nonslip _____ on the floor. Don't forget to put that
       f.
slippery soap back in the _____ after you wash.
            g.
Provide a stool so that children can reach the _____ safely to wash their hands
                 h.
and brush their teeth.

4. Keep medicines locked in the _____ . Never throw old medicines away in a
             i.
_____ where children can get them. Flush them down the _____ .
  j.   **k.**

Based on information from: Larson, D.: _Mayo Clinic Family Health Book._ (NY: William Morrow and Company, 1990)

3. What about you? What do you do to prevent injuries and accidents in the bathroom? Write
sentences on your own paper.

Example: _We put a rubber mat in the bathtub._

Challenge List items in a bathroom that usually cost $10.00 or less.

A Bedroom

1. Look in your dictionary. **True** or **False**? Correct the underlined words in the false sentences.

   a. The ~~flat sheet~~ *pillow* is striped.   _____False_____

   b. The clock radio is on the <u>bureau</u>.   _____

   c. The <u>light switch</u> and the outlet are on the same wall.   _____

   d. There is a <u>mirror</u> over the bed.   _____

   e. The woman is lifting the <u>bedspread</u> and the dust ruffle.   _____

2. Read the letter and look at the picture. Complete Tran's list on your own paper.

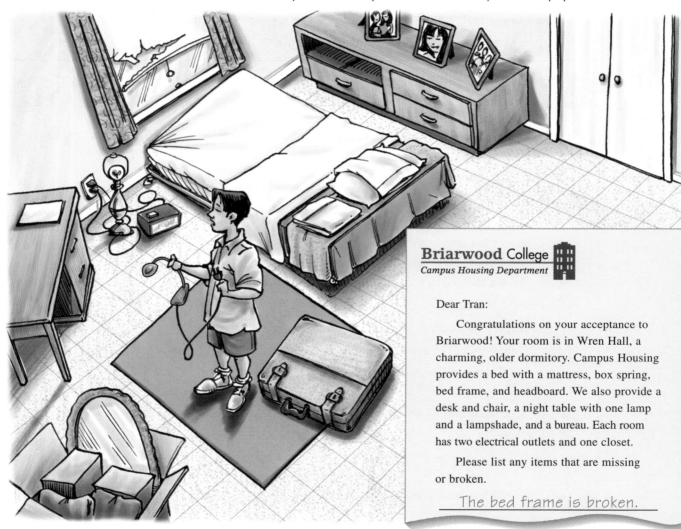

Briarwood College
Campus Housing Department

Dear Tran:

Congratulations on your acceptance to Briarwood! Your room is in Wren Hall, a charming, older dormitory. Campus Housing provides a bed with a mattress, box spring, bed frame, and headboard. We also provide a desk and chair, a night table with one lamp and a lampshade, and a bureau. Each room has two electrical outlets and one closet.

Please list any items that are missing or broken.

The bed frame is broken.

3. Look at Exercise 2. What did Tran bring? Make a list on your own paper.

   Example: *sheets*

Challenge Write a paragraph describing your ideal bedroom.

44

1. Look in your dictionary. Cross out the word that doesn't belong. Write the category. Use the words in the box. (You will use one word more than once.)

	safety	**storage**	**playing**	~~**sleeping**~~
a. ___sleeping___	crib	~~puzzle~~	bunk bed	cradle
b. _____	baby monitor	smoke detector	bumper pad	blocks
c. _____	changing table	chest of drawers	toy chest	picture book
d. _____	ball	diaper pail	doll	teddy bear
e. _____	coloring book	dollhouse	crayons	comforter

2. Complete the article. Use the words in the box.

mobile	changing table	wallpaper	stuffed animals	~~crib~~
comforter	chest of drawers	diaper pail	night-light	

Expecting a new family member? Here's what you'll need to make your baby's room a safe and happy place. The biggest item is the ___crib___ . The mattress must
a.
fit tightly, with no spaces that a baby's head can fit through. A pretty _____ will
b.
keep baby warm, but it should fit loosely on top of the mattress. You can change your
baby on a bed, but a _____ is better for your back. You can keep diapers on
c.
the shelves below. Have a _____ nearby for the dirty ones. Finally, you will need
d.
a _____ for baby's clothing and extra blankets.
e.
    For decoration, hang a _____ where baby can watch it (some play music, too).
f.
Paint the room or put up colorful _____ , add some lovable _____ to
g. **h.**
hug, and plug a cheerful _____ into an electrical outlet for nighttime feedings.
i.

3. What about you? Describe your favorite toy or game as a child.

Example: *When I was three, I loved my little teddy bear.*

_____

Challenge Look at **page 183** in this book. Follow the instructions.

Housework

1. Look in your dictionary. Correct the underlined words in these false sentences.

                       cleaning

  a. The woman in C is ~~emptying~~ the oven.   **c.** The girl in N is <u>washing</u> the dishes.

  b. The man in L is <u>polishing</u> the floor.   **d.** The man in J is <u>sweeping</u> the floor.

2. Look at the room. Circle the correct words to complete the note.

Hi! As you can see, I wasn't quite able to do everything. I polished the **desk** / dresser,
a.
but I didn't have a chance to dust the
desk / dresser. I **swept / vacuumed** the floor,
b.   **c.**
and I finally washed the **dishes / windows**.
d.
I also washed the **sheets / glasses**, but
e.
didn't make **lunch / the bed**. Sorry! By the
f.
way, could you **take out / empty** the garbage
g.
and put away the **dishes / books**?
h.

Thanks. See you after class,
Viktor

3. What about you? Which would you rather do? Write sentences on your own paper.

  a. wash the dishes / dry the dishes   **c.** sweep the floor / vacuum the carpet

  b. dust the furniture / polish the furniture   **d.** clean the oven / wash the windows

  Example: *I'd rather dry the dishes than wash the dishes.*

Challenge Take a survey. Ask five people about their favorite and least favorite kinds of housework. Write their answers.

46

1. Look in your dictionary. Add a word to complete the list of cleaning supplies.

a. dust _____ *mop* _____   e. recycling _____

b. rubber _____   f. scrub _____

c. trash _____   g. vacuum _____

d. dish _____   h. furniture _____

2. Complete the conversations. Use the words from Exercise 1.

a. **Ben:** Water isn't good for the dining room floor, is it?

Ann: No. Use the _____ *dust mop* _____.

b. **Paulo:** Do you have any _____? I want to empty the wastebasket.

Sara: Oh. I used the last one.

c. **Ada:** The _____ doesn't seem to be working well.

Mario: Maybe the bag is full. Have you checked it?

d. **Fei-mei:** If you give me a _____, I'll dry the dishes.

Da-ming: Great.

e. **Luis:** You know, that cleanser isn't good for your hands.

Vera: You're right. Do we have any _____?

f. **Taro:** What should we do with the empty bottles?

Rika: Don't throw them away. Put them in the _____ in the alley.

g. **Amber:** I dusted the desk, but it still doesn't look clean.

Chet: Try some _____ on it.

h. **Layla:** The kitchen floor is really dirty.

Zaki: I know. You have to get down and use the _____ on it.

3. Cross out the word that doesn't belong. Give a reason.

a. dustpan   broom   ~~glass cleaner~~   wet mop
   You don't use it to clean the floor. _____

b. steel-wool soap pads   dishwashing liquid   dish towel   bucket
   _____

c. scrub brush   sponge   feather duster   wet mop
   _____

Challenge Imagine you have just moved into a new home. What do you need to: dust the furniture, clean the oven, wash the windows, mop the kitchen floor? Make a shopping list. You can use your dictionary for help.

1. Look in your dictionary. Who should they call?

a.  A toy is stuck in the toilet.

<u>the plumber</u>

c. My front door key isn't working.

_____

b. I think that hailstorm did some damage. There's a water stain on the ceiling.

_____

d. WISCONSIN America's Dairyland — Sorry, Mom. I kicked my soccer ball through the front window.

_____

2. Look at Tracy and Kyung's cabin. Complete the telephone conversations by describing the problem or problems for each repair service.

a. **Repairperson:** Bob Derby Carpentry. Can I help you?
   Tracy: <u>The door on our kitchen cabinet is broken</u> .

b. **Repairperson:** Plumbing Specialists, Ron here.
   Kyung: _____ ,
   _____ , and
   _____ .

c. **Repairperson:** Quick Fixes Small Repairs. What can we do for you?
   Tracy: _____ .

d. **Repairperson:** Chestertown Electricians. This is Pat.
   Kyung: _____ .

e. **Repairperson:** Nature's Way Exterminators. What's the problem?
   Tracy: _____ !

3. Look at the chart. **True** or **False**? Write a question mark (**?**) if the information isn't in the chart.

Pests	Where They Live	How to Prevent Them	How to Get Rid of Them
	on pets, carpets, furniture	Keep pets either inside or outside all the time.	Vacuum often. Comb pets daily. Wash them with water and lemon juice.
	behind walls, under roofs and floors	Repair cracks and holes in roofs and walls. Keep garbage in tightly closed garbage cans.	Poison is dangerous to humans. Put traps along walls instead. Put a piece of bacon in the trap.
	in wood; especially wet or damaged places	Repair cracks and holes. Repair leaks in pipes. Check every 1–2 years.	Call the exterminator. You need a professional to get rid of these pests, which destroy your house by eating the wood.
	gardens and lawns	Repair wall cracks. Clean floors and shelves often; wipe spilled honey or jam immediately.	Find where they enter the house and repair that hole. Put mint leaves in food cupboards.
	behind walls, in electric appliances	Clean carefully; keep food in closed containers. Repair all cracks and holes.	Make a trap by putting a banana in a wide-mouthed jar. Put petroleum jelly around the inside of jar to keep trapped bugs inside. Place in corners or under sinks.

a. To prevent most pests, you must repair household problems. ____True____

b. You have to use poison to get rid of mice and rats. _____

c. Sometimes cockroaches get into the toaster oven. _____

d. Fleas like sweet food. _____

e. You have to buy cockroach traps. _____

f. Ants carry diseases. _____

g. Mint leaves help get rid of termites. _____

h. Termites are very common in warm, wet climates. _____

i. Mice eat people's food. _____

j. You should put a piece of fruit in a mousetrap. _____

Challenge Write some other ways of dealing with household pests.

▶ **Go to page 172 for Another Look (Unit 3).**

Fruit

1. Look in your dictionary. Complete each statement.

   a. Two pints of ___blueberries___ cost $3.98.

   b. The man is hanging a basket of _____.

   c. The green banana is _____.

   d. The _____ banana has brown spots.

2. Look at the pictures. Complete the chart with the names of the fruit.

   Buying fresh fruit is an art. Here are some tips:

Fruit		Best During	Buy Ones That Are
	a. ___watermelon___	June, July, August	cut open, dark red inside
	b. _____	June and July	dark red and big
	c. _____	July and August	bright orange, with soft skins
	d. _____	December–June	heavy
	e. _____	the whole year	not soft (Let them get ripe at home.)
	f. _____	April 15–July 15	dry and dark red (Size is not important.)
	g. _____	July and August	dark green

   Based on information from: Murdich, J.: *Buying Produce: The Greengrocer's Guide to Selecting and Storing Fresh Fruits and Vegetables.* (NY: Hearst Marine Books, 1986)

3. Look at Exercise 2. **True** or **False**? Write a question mark (**?**) if the information isn't in the chart.

   a. The best mangoes are very heavy.   ___?___

   b. Don't buy a watermelon unless it has been cut open.   _____

   c. Raspberries become rotten very quickly.   _____

   d. Small strawberries taste better.   _____

   e. Fresh apples are best in the summer.   _____

   f. The best juice oranges come from Florida.   _____

   g. When you buy cherries, size is important.   _____

   h. You should buy avocadoes that are completely ripe.   _____

   i. Summer is a good time to buy lemons.   _____

   j. Apricots should be bright orange when you buy them.   _____

   k. A ripe cantaloupe is soft at both ends.   _____

4. What about you? List your favorite fruits. When do you buy them? Use your own paper.

Challenge Make a chart like the one in Exercise 2 for your favorite fruits.

1. Look in your dictionary. Put these vegetables in the correct category.

lettuce	spinach	carrots	zucchini	~~radishes~~	corn	parsley
~~chili peppers~~	squash	turnips	eggplants	cucumbers		string beans
beets	tomatoes	sweet peppers	cabbage	peas	yams	~~artichokes~~

ROOT VEGETABLES   **LEAF VEGETABLES**   **VEGETABLES WITH SEEDS**

radishes   _artichokes_   _chili peppers_   _____

_____   _____   _____   _____

_____   _____   _____   _____

_____   _____   _____   _____

_____   _____   _____   _____

2. Complete the recipe with the amounts and names of the vegetables in the picture. (Look at **page 58** in your dictionary for ways to prepare foods.)

HEALTHY VEGETABLE STEW

Put three cups of water on the stove to boil. While it is heating, use a sharp knife to slice

_____ _four_ _____ _potatoes_ _____, _____ _____,
    a.   **b.**

_____ _____, and _____ _____.
    c.   **d.**

Cut _____ _____ into quarters, and crush four cloves of
        e.

_____ with the back of a spoon. Add these ingredients to the boiling water and
    f.

cook over low heat for 20 minutes. Add _____ cups of _____
                                            g.   **h.**

and cook for three more minutes.

3. What about you? Check (✔) the ways you like to eat vegetables.

VEGETABLE	STIR-FRIED	SAUTÉED	STEAMED	BAKED	BOILED	RAW
broccoli						
cauliflower						
scallions						
mushrooms						
Other: _____						

Challenge Write the recipe for a vegetable dish.

Meat and Poultry

1. Look in your dictionary. Cross out the word that doesn't belong. Write the category.

a. ___poultry___	~~bacon~~	breast	thigh	wing
b. _____	sausage	bacon	chop	tripe
c. _____	leg	chop	wing	shank
d. _____	liver	gizzard	tripe	steak

2. Complete the article with information from the charts.

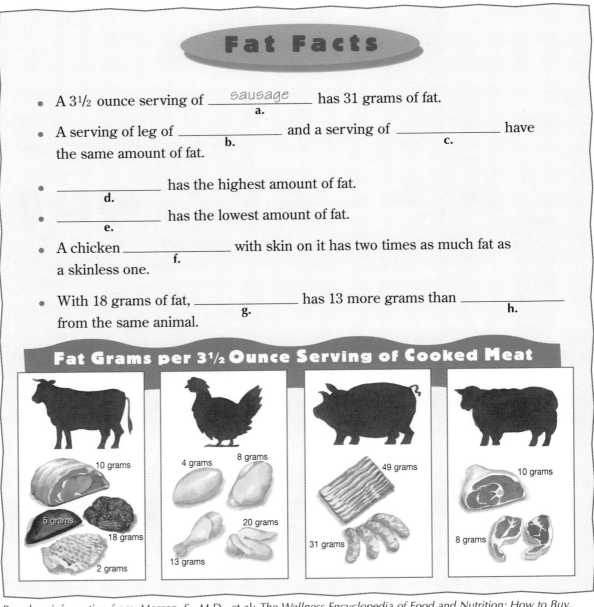

Fat Facts

- A 3½ ounce serving of ___sausage___ has 31 grams of fat.
  a.

- A serving of leg of _____ and a serving of _____ have
  b.   **c.**
  the same amount of fat.

- _____ has the highest amount of fat.
  d.

- _____ has the lowest amount of fat.
  e.

- A chicken _____ with skin on it has two times as much fat as
  f.
  a skinless one.

- With 18 grams of fat, _____ has 13 more grams than _____
  g.   **h.**
  from the same animal.

Fat Grams per 3½ Ounce Serving of Cooked Meat

10 grams
5 grams
18 grams
2 grams

4 grams
8 grams
20 grams
13 grams

49 grams
31 grams

10 grams
8 grams

Based on information from: Margen, S., M.D., et al: *The Wellness Encyclopedia of Food and Nutrition: How to Buy, Store, and Prepare Every Variety of Fresh Food.* (NY: Random House, 1992.)

Challenge Keep a record of the meat you eat in one day. Figure out the fat content. Use the
information in Exercise 2.

1. Look in your dictionary. **True** or **False**? Correct the underlined words in the false sentences.

   potato salad
   a. There's a spoon in the ~~pasta salad~~.   _False_

   b. Salami is <u>meat</u>.   _____

   c. The potato salad is next to the <u>cheddar cheese</u>.   _____

   d. The Swiss cheese is between the cheddar cheese
   and the <u>American cheese</u>.   _____

   e. The <u>rye bread</u> has seeds in it.   _____

   f. There are some <u>whole halibut</u> for sale.   _____

   g. The trout is <u>frozen</u>.   _____

   h. The <u>sole</u> has no bones.   _____

2. Look at the seafood prices and the recipe cards. How much will the seafood for each recipe cost? (See dictionary **page 57** for information about weights and measures.)

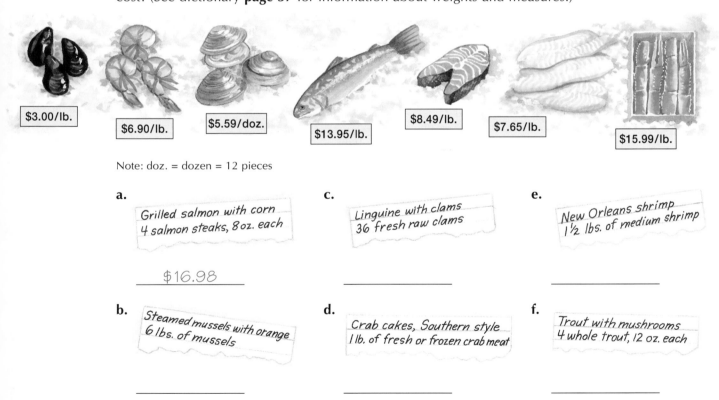

$3.00/lb. $6.90/lb. $5.59/doz. $13.95/lb. $8.49/lb. $7.65/lb. $15.99/lb.

Note: doz. = dozen = 12 pieces

a.
Grilled salmon with corn
4 salmon steaks, 8 oz. each

_$16.98_

b.
Steamed mussels with orange
6 lbs. of mussels

_____

c.
Linguine with clams
36 fresh raw clams

_____

d.
Crab cakes, Southern style
1 lb. of fresh or frozen crab meat

_____

e.
New Orleans shrimp
1½ lbs. of medium shrimp

_____

f.
Trout with mushrooms
4 whole trout, 12 oz. each

_____

3. What about you? Order lunch from the deli for yourself and a friend. Use your own paper.

   Example: *One ham and cheddar cheese sandwich on wheat bread with a side order of coleslaw.*
   One turkey breast on white bread.

Challenge Plan a party menu for your class. Use a deli menu and the information from Exercise 2.
How much will you buy? How much will it cost?

The Market

1. Look in your dictionary. Cross out the word that doesn't belong. Write the section of the store.

a. _canned goods_	soup	~~sugar~~	beans	tuna
b. _____	bananas	tomatoes	oranges	rolls
c. _____	yogurt	eggs	milk	ice cream
d. _____	soda	bottled water	sour cream	apple juice
e. _____	rice	bread	cake	cookies
f. _____	butter	gum	potato chips	candy bars
g. _____	chicken	cheese	turkey	steak
h. _____	oil	flour	spaghetti	cake mix
i. _____	aluminum foil	plastic wrap	paper towels	pet food

2. Complete the article. Use the words in the box.

bagger	**basket**	**beans**	**bottle return**	**cart**	**cash register**
checker	**checkstands**	**coffee**	~~**cookies**~~	**line**	**manager**
	margarine	**paper**	**plastic**	**produce**	**vegetables**

SAVE TIME AND MONEY: Some Shopping Tips

- Never shop when you're hungry. Those chocolate _____cookies_____ will be hard
  a.

  to resist on an empty stomach.

- Do you really need a large shopping _____, or is a smaller shopping
  b.

  _____ enough? Having too much room may encourage you to buy
  c.

  more than you need.

- Shop with a list. That makes it easier to buy only what you need.

- Keep a price book of items that you buy frequently. *Example:* If you drink a lot of

  _____, compare prices at different stores.
  d.

- Always check the unit price. *Example:* It may be cheaper to buy a large can of

  _____ than a small can. The important question: How much does it
  e.

  cost *per pound?*

- Watch for sales. Buy a lot of the items you need.

- Buy the store brand. *Example:* A container of Supermarket Brand _____
  f.
  will probably cost less than the famous brands.

- If the _____ doesn't look fresh, buy frozen _____.
  g.   h.
  They'll look and taste better.

- Avoid standing in _____. Try to shop when the store is less crowded.
  i.
  If all the _____ aren't open, speak to the store _____.
  j.   k.

- Always watch the _____ when the _____ is ringing
  l.   m.
  up your order. Is the price the same as the one on the item? Mistakes can happen!

- Don't throw away those empty cola bottles without looking! In some states, you
  can get a refund. Take them to the _____.
  n.

- If the _____ gives you a choice between a _____ or
  o.   p.
  _____ bag, consider paper—it can be recycled. If the store only has
  q.
  plastic bags, use them again!

3. What about you? Which of the shopping tips in Exercise 2 do you follow? Which ones will you try? What other ways do you save money when you go food shopping? Write about them. Use your own paper.

Challenge Make a list of ten food items that you often buy. Go to two stores and compare prices.
Example:

Item

1. can of beans

Store A: Shop & Save / Item Size: 15 oz. / Price: $.99 / Unit Price: $1.05 per lb.

Store B: B&D / Item Size: 19 oz. / Price: $1.09 / Unit Price: $.91 per lb.

2. _____

Store A: _____ / Item Size: _____ / Price: _____ / Unit Price: _____

Store B: _____ / Item Size: _____ / Price: _____ / Unit Price: _____

Containers and Packaged Foods

1. Look in your dictionary. Complete the flyer.

RECYCLE—It's the Law!

The packaging for many items on your grocery list belongs in your recycling bin, not your garbage can.
Follow the recycling guidelines as you use these items.

YES

a. ☑ plastic or glass ____bottles____ (soda, juice)

b. ☑ plastic or glass _____ (jam)

c. ☑ plastic _____ (yogurt)

d. ☑ cardboard _____ (eggs, milk)

e. ☑ metal _____ (tuna, soup)

NO

f. ☒ plastic ____bags____ (bread)

g. ☒ cardboard _____ (cereal)

h. ☒ cardboard _____ (paper towels)

i. ☒ plastic _____ (cookies)

j. ☒ plastic _____ (toothpaste)

Note: Recycling guidelines are different in different places.

2. Look at the groceries that Mee-Yon bought this week. Which items have packaging that she can recycle? Which items don't? Complete the lists below. Use information from Exercise 1.

Recycle packaging for...

YES	NO
a bottle of oil	2 loaves of bread

3. What about you? Look in your refrigerator and kitchen cupboards. List items that you can and can't recycle. Use information from Exercise 1.

Challenge   Where are the recycling centers in your community? What kinds of containers does each one accept?

1. Look at the charts in your dictionary. Circle the larger amount.

   a. 3 teaspoons / (3 tablespoons)   **d.** 2 pints / 1 liter

   b. 100 milliliters / 2 fluid ounces   **e.** 2 pounds / 36 ounces

   c. 8 pints / 6 quarts   **f.** 5 quarts / 2 gallons

2. Look at the nutrition facts. Answer the questions. Use your dictionary for help.

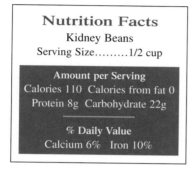

Nutrition Facts
Kidney Beans
Serving Size.........1/2 cup

Amount per Serving
Calories 110 Calories from fat 0
Protein 8g Carbohydrate 22g

% Daily Value
Calcium 6% Iron 10%

Skim Milk
Nutrition Facts
Serving Size 1 cup

Amount per Serving
Calories 90   Calories from fat 0
Protein 8g

% Daily Value
Calcium 30%   Vitamin D 25%

Nutrition Facts
Rice
Serving Size 1/4 cup raw (about 1 cup cooked)

Amount per Serving
Calories 170   Calories from fat 0
Protein 4 grams   Carbohydrate 38 grams

% Daily Value
Calcium.......... 2%   Iron.............. 8%

CHOCOLATE CANDY
Nutrition Facts
Serving Size 1 piece (1/2 oz.)
AMOUNT PER SERVING
Calories 90   Calories from fat 30
Total fat 4g • Protein 1g

Note: g = grams   % Daily Value = % of the total amount you should have in one day

   a. Which has more protein, a cup of beans or a cup of milk?   _a cup of beans_

   b. How many pieces of chocolate candy are there in one pound?   _____

   c. How many pints of milk give 100% of the daily value of Vitamin D?   _____

   d. How much fat is there in three ounces of chocolate candy?   _____

   e. A serving of rice and beans contains a quarter cup of beans and a half cup of cooked rice. How much carbohydrate is there in a serving?   _____

   f. What percent of the daily value of iron is there in a serving of rice and beans?   _____

   g. How many gallons of milk do you need for 32 servings?   _____

   h. What percent of the daily value of calcium do you get from a pint of milk and two servings of rice?   _____

Challenge Look at **page 184** in this book. Follow the instructions.

Food Preparation

1. Look in your dictionary. Complete the cookbook definitions. (*Hint:* The words are in alphabetical order.)

   a. _____bake_____ : Cook by dry heat in an oven. (cake, potatoes)

   b. _____ : Cook over an open fire with a sauce brushed on, often outside.

   c. _____ : Make mixture smooth by quick motion with a spoon, fork, or whisk. (eggs)

   d. _____ : Cook in very hot liquid (212°F for water).

   e. _____ : Cook in contact with direct heat under the broiler.

   f. _____ : Cut into pieces with a knife or other sharp tool.

   g. _____ : Cook in hot oil in a large pot or pan.

   h. _____ : Cut into very small pieces using small holes of a grater. (cheese)

   i. _____ : See *barbecue*.

   j. _____ : Combine ingredients, usually with a spoon.

   k. _____ : Take off outer covering. (onion, carrot)

   l. _____ : Cook in a small amount of hot butter or oil. (onion, garlic)

   m. _____ : Cook slowly in liquid just below the boiling point.

   n. _____ : Cook over boiling water, not in it. (vegetables)

2. Look at Andy's recipe. It got wet, and now he can't read parts of it. Complete the recipe. Use the words in the box.

add	bake	~~grease~~	mix	pour	slice

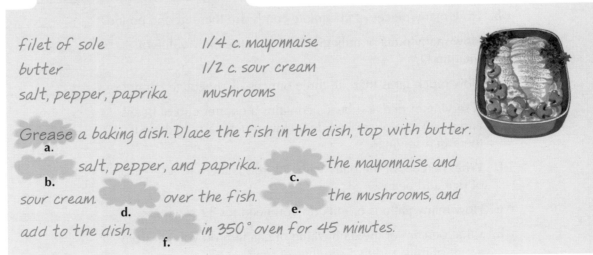

   Baked sole in sour cream

   filet of sole   1/4 c. mayonnaise
   butter   1/2 c. sour cream
   salt, pepper, paprika mushrooms

   Grease a baking dish. Place the fish in the dish, top with butter.
   a.
   _____ salt, pepper, and paprika. _____ the mayonnaise and
   b.   c.
   sour cream. _____ over the fish. _____ the mushrooms, and
   d.   e.
   add to the dish. _____ in 350° oven for 45 minutes.
   f.

Challenge Write one of your favorite recipes.

1. Look in your dictionary. **True** or **False**? Correct the <u>underlined</u> words in the false sentences.

                                  counter

   a. There's a casserole dish on the ~~stove~~.   *False*

   b. One of the cooks is using a <u>can opener</u>.   _____

   c. Another cook is putting <u>pasta</u> into a colander.   _____

   d. The cook with the rolling pin is making a <u>pie</u>.   _____

   e. One of the cooks used the <u>vegetable peeler</u>.   _____

   f. There's a <u>turkey</u> in the roasting pan.   _____

   g. There are five <u>rolls</u> on the cookie sheet.   _____

   h. There's <u>butter</u> in the frying pan.   _____

2. Circle the correct words to complete the cookbook information.

Some utensils you need in your kitchen:

   a. **Grater /(Whisk):** for beating eggs, cream, etc.

   b. **Steamer / Colander:** for removing water from cooked pasta, vegetables, etc.

   c. **Ladle / Spatula:** for spooning soup, sauces, etc., out of a pot

   d. **Paring / Carving knife:** for cutting up small fruits and vegetables

   e. **Tongs / Lids:** for covering pots and pans

   f. **Plastic storage containers / Strainers:** for keeping food fresh

   g. **Pots / Pot holders:** for handling hot utensils

   h. **Eggbeaters / Wooden spoons:** for stirring soup, sauces, etc.

   i. **Double boiler / Roasting rack:** for slow cooking on top of the stove

   j. **Cake and pie pans / pins:** for baking desserts

Challenge Look in your dictionary. Make a list of the five most important kitchen utensils. Explain your choices.

1. Look in your dictionary. Where can you hear…?

a. "How's your taco?"   ___booth___

b. "I'll have a hamburger with fries, and a large soda."   _____

c. "After this hot dog, I'm going to the salad bar."   _____

2. Look at the chart. **True** or **False**? Write a question mark (**?**) if the information isn't there.

Based on information from: Choron, S. and H.: *The Book of Lists for Kids.* (NY: Houghton Mifflin Co., 1995)

a. Hot dogs are the most popular food.   ___False___

b. Cheeseburgers are more popular than hamburgers.   _____

c. French fries are among the ten most popular foods.   _____

d. Muffins are more popular than doughnuts.   _____

e. Pizza is more popular than spaghetti.   _____

f. Nachos are one of the top ten fast food items.   _____

g. Frozen yogurt is very popular.   _____

3. Match the ingredients labels with the condiments.

___3___ **a.** INGREDIENTS: VINEGAR, MUSTARD SEED, SALT, TURMERIC

_____ **b.** INGREDIENTS: SOYBEAN OIL, WHOLE EGGS, VINEGAR, WATER, EGG YOLKS, SALT, SUGAR, LEMON JUICE, NATURAL FLAVORINGS

_____ **c.** INGREDIENTS: CUCUMBERS, CORN SYRUP, VINEGAR, ONIONS, WATER, SALT, SUGAR, SPICES, PEPPERS

_____ **d.** ■ INGREDIENTS: TOMATO CONCENTRATE (WATER, TOMATO PASTE), CORN SYRUP, VINEGAR, SALT, SPICES

1. ketchup

2. mayonnaise

3. mustard

4. relish

4. What about you? List your "top ten" fast foods. Use your own paper.

Challenge Take a survey of your classmates' top ten fast foods.

1. Look in your dictionary. Cross out the word that doesn't belong. Write the category.

    a. _____desserts_____   pudding   ~~mashed potatoes~~   pie   cake

    b. _____   garlic bread   waffles   scrambled eggs   pancakes

    c. _____   coffee   decaf coffee   syrup   tea

    d. _____   chef's salad   sandwich   sausage   soup

    e. _____   bacon   pasta   baked potato   fried fish

2. Look at the pictures. Circle the correct words to complete one of the orders.

"I'll have pasta / (soup),   steak / a chef's salad , and a cup of coffee / tea."
             a.   **b.**   **c.**

"I'd like fried fish / roast chicken with mashed potatoes / rice pilaf , and a cup of tea / coffee.
                  d.   **e.**   **f.**

Pudding / Pie for dessert, please."
    g.

"I'll have pancakes / waffles and ice cream / syrup with bacon / sausage and a cup of
             h.   **i.**   **j.**

tea / decaf coffee ."
    k.

3. Look again at the pictures in Exercise 2. Write the *other* orders in the correct category.

    a. Breakfast: "I'll have _scrambled eggs, toast, and a cup of coffee_ ____."

    b. Lunch: "I'd like _____."

    c. Dinner: "I'll have _____."

4. What about you? Order a meal from Exercise 2.

_____.

Challenge   Imagine you own a coffee shop. Write your own menu.

1. Look at the top picture on pages 62 and 63 in your dictionary. Who said…?

a. "Your table will be ready in a minute, Mr. and Mrs. Pyle."   _hostess_

b. "Would you like spinach or broccoli with that?"   _____

c. "This salad is delicious."   _____

d. "We also have chocolate, coconut, and mango ice cream."   _____

e. "Here are some more dirty dishes!"   _____

f. "The glasses are all clean, and I'm almost done with these plates."   _____

2. Circle the correct words to complete this restaurant review.

☆☆☆

A.J. Clarke's   290 Park Place   555-3454

As soon as I walked into Clarke's, I was impressed by the handsome pink and green (dining room) / kitchen that can serve about
a.
50 chefs / diners. The hostess seated / served my
b.   **c.**
guest and me at a quiet table in the corner where we immediately got a bread basket / soup bowl
d.
filled with warm, freshly baked rolls. The service was great. The patron / busperson continued to
e.
pour / clear water throughout the meal.
f.
And what a meal it was! The bill / menu
g.
had something for everyone. Our

dishwasher / server, Todd, recommended the fish
h.
of the day, tuna. My friend ordered / served the
i.
chicken l'orange. After Todd carried / took our
j.
orders, he brought us two salad forks / plates
k.
with the freshest lettuce I've ever eaten.

This was followed by two large—and delicious— bowls / plates of onion soup. Our main dishes did
l.
not disappoint us. The tuna was so tender that you could cut it without the steak knife / teaspoon that
m.
came with it. The chicken, too, was wonderful.

When we were finished, the busperson cleared / set the table. Time for dessert! Todd
n.
carried / left out the dessert fork / tray, which was
o.   **p.**
filled with several cakes and pies—all baked in the restaurant's own kitchen / dishroom. Raspberry
q.
pie with whipped cream and a cup / saucer of
r.
delicious hot coffee ended our perfect meal.

We happily paid / poured our check and left / took
s.   **t.**
Todd a nice tip. My tip to you: Eat at A.J. Clarke's.

Reservations recommended.

3. Look at the picture and complete the description.

$\mathcal{A}$ formal _____place setting_____
a.

A _____ is in the center, usually with the _____
b.   c.

on top of it. The flatware is on both sides. To the left of the plate are

(from closest to farthest) a _____ and a _____.
d.   e.

To the right of the plate are a _____, a _____,
f.   g.

and sometimes a shellfish _____. Above and to the right
h.

of the plate are a _____ and two _____.
i.   j.

There is also a small _____ above and to the left
k.

of the dinner plate. The butter _____ is set on top of it.
l.

4. What about you? Most people's table settings do not look like the formal one in Exercise 3! Draw your table setting. How is it the same? How is it different? Write sentences on your own paper.

Example: *We put the napkin under the fork.*

Challenge Write a description of a meal you had at a restaurant or at someone's home.

▶ **Go to page 173 for Another Look (Unit 4).**

Clothing I

1. Look in your dictionary. Who said…? Identify the people by their clothes.

   a. "Only one more mile."

      <u>The man in the sweatshirt and sweatpants.</u>

   b. "You look so good in your new turtleneck."

      _____

   c. "It's 6:05. Where's the bus?"

      _____

   d. "Mommy, can Ricky and I sit in the first row?"

      _____

   e. "Your tickets, please."

      _____

   f. "You look nice in that dress."

      _____

   g. "Where's the women's rest room, please?"

      _____

   h. "Daddy, look there!"

      _____

   i. "Here's the last letter."

      _____

2. Circle the correct words to complete the article.

Back to Basics

Building a basic wardrobe? Here are a few items of clothing that you can wear almost anywhere—from a job interview to a walk in the park.

FOR MEN:

A navy blue (suit) / tuxedo. Wear it with a white   shirt / knit shirt
       a.   **b.**

for formal occasions.

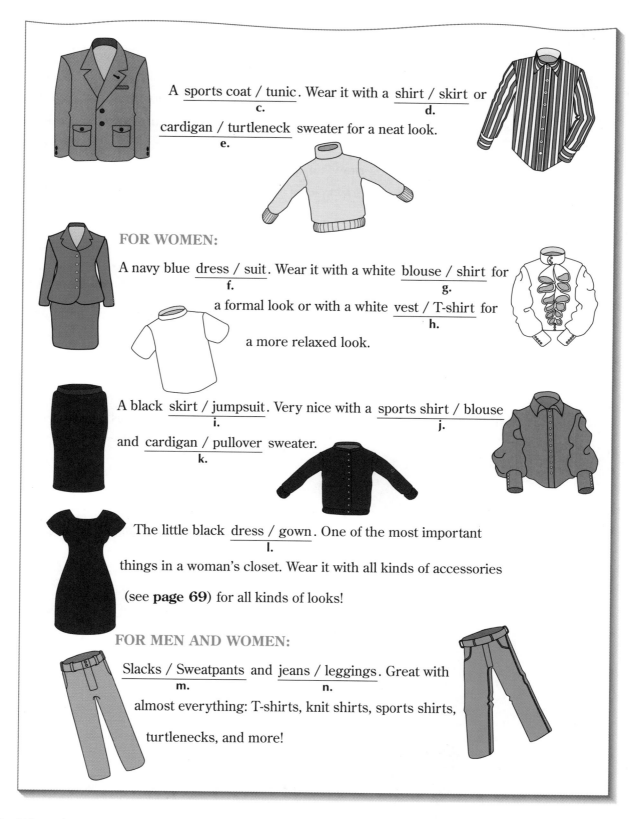

A <u>sports coat / tunic</u>. Wear it with a <u>shirt / skirt</u> or
         c.   **d.**

<u>cardigan / turtleneck</u> sweater for a neat look.
         e.

FOR WOMEN:

A navy blue <u>dress / suit</u>. Wear it with a white <u>blouse / shirt</u> for
               f.   **g.**

a formal look or with a white <u>vest / T-shirt</u> for
                             h.

a more relaxed look.

A black <u>skirt / jumpsuit</u>. Very nice with a <u>sports shirt / blouse</u>
       i.   **j.**

and <u>cardigan / pullover</u> sweater.
     k.

The little black <u>dress / gown</u>. One of the most important
             l.

things in a woman's closet. Wear it with all kinds of accessories

(see **page 69**) for all kinds of looks!

FOR MEN AND WOMEN:

<u>Slacks / Sweatpants</u> and <u>jeans / leggings</u>. Great with
        m.   **n.**

almost everything: T-shirts, knit shirts, sports shirts,

turtlenecks, and more!

3. What about you? What do you think are the most important items of clothing to have? Where do
you wear these clothes?

Example: *slacks and a sports shirt—I wear them to work, to school, and at home.*

Challenge Choose five people from your dictionary. Describe their clothes. **Example:** *The
administrative assistant on page 136 is wearing a blue skirt and a pink blouse.*

Clothing II

1. Look in your dictionary. Cross out the word that doesn't belong. Write the weather condition.

   a. ___raining___ poncho rain boots umbrella ~~ski hat~~

   b. _____ overcoat cover-up muffler jacket

   c. _____ straw hat bathing suit parka sunglasses

   d. _____ down jacket tights ski mask baseball cap

2. Correct the ad.

   It's windy out there, but Jillian is dressed for the weather in a
   warm brown leather ~~parka~~ *jacket*, bright red earmuffs, and a red and
   yellow muffler. That straw hat protects her from the autumn wind.

   Jillian

3. Write ads for Abdulla, Polly, and Julio's clothing. Use Exercise 2 as a model.

   Abdulla

   a. _____
   _____
   _____

   Polly

   b. _____
   _____
   _____

   Julio

   c. _____
   _____
   _____

Challenge What do you like to wear in different weather conditions? Write short paragraphs like the ones in Exercise 3.

1. Look in your dictionary. Find the words that complete *a pair of....*

<u> bike shorts </u>   _____   _____   _____

_____   _____   _____   _____

_____   _____   _____

2. Read the note. Then complete each list with the correct name and items to pack. Continue on your own paper.

> *Dear Ann,*
>
>   *Thanks for agreeing to take care of Bobby this weekend. I have to go out of town, and Julio is going skiing. Inga can't baby-sit because she's going on a bike trip. We appreciate your help!*
>
>   *Love,*
>
>   *Amanda*

a. for *Bobby*
     two blanket sleepers

b. for _____

c. for _____

d. for _____

Challenge   You're going on a trip next weekend. List the underwear and sleepwear you'll take.

Shoes and Accessories

1. Look at items 25–43 on **page 69** in your dictionary. Read the sentences. Write the names of the items the people are talking about.

   a. "I always keep my coins in <u>one</u>—separate from my bills." _change purse_

   b. "According to this <u>one</u>, it's 8:20." _____

   c. "What does the *NJ* on <u>it</u> stand for?" _____

   d. "Ow! <u>This</u> is sharp! I just stabbed myself with it." _____

   e. "Wow! <u>This</u> has even more room than the backpack!" _____

   f. "John gave <u>one</u> to me. I put his photo in it." _____

   g. "Oh, no. I forgot to put my credit card back in <u>it</u>." _____

2. Complete the ad.

Newport Mall—*Your one stop for fall fashions!*

Men's green and purple _____tie_____
a.

▶ The Neck Stop

Black _____ and silver _____
b. **c.**

▶ Accessories East

Blue and yellow _____
d.

▶ Foot Smart

Gold _____ and
e.

pierced _____
f.

▶ E.R. Jewelers

Red _____
g.

▶ The Bag House

3. Look at the shopping list. Where can you buy these items? Use the stores from Exercise 2.

To buy –
bow tie _____The Neck Stop_____
brown purse _____
gold bracelet _____
backpack _____
pearls _____
black boots _____

4. Circle the correct words to complete this card.

If the Shoe Fits

Always try on shoes / scarves at the end of the day—your feet are bigger then!
a.
Ask yourself: Is there enough room at the sole / toe? There should be at least
b.
1/2" between the end of your foot and the beginning of the shoe. And remember,

you need different kinds of shoes for different kinds of activities. Women may want

to wear high heels / oxfords to an evening party, but tennis shoes / pumps are a
c. **d.**
better choice for the office. The lower the heel / pin, the more comfortable the
e.
shoe. Both women and men can relax at home in a pair of hiking boots / loafers,
f.
but you'll want shoes with belts / shoelaces for walking. And if running is part of
g.
your daily routine, athletic shoes / sandals are the best bet.
h.

Foot Smart at the Newport Mall

5. What about you? How do you feel about…? Circle the number that's true for you.

	LIKE ←			→ DON'T LIKE	
a. high heel shoes	1	2	3	4	5
b. hats	1	2	3	4	5
c. suspenders	1	2	3	4	5
d. bow ties	1	2	3	4	5
e. pierced earrings	1	2	3	4	5

Challenge Which accessories make good gifts? Explain who you would buy them for and why.
Example: *I'd buy a backpack for my girlfriend because she loves to hike.*

69

Describing Clothes

1. Look in your dictionary. Cross out the word that doesn't belong. Write the category.

   a. <u>sweater styles</u>   V-neck   crewneck   ~~casual~~   turtleneck
   b. _____   nylon   plaid   paisley   polka-dotted
   c. _____   large   extra large   small   too small
   d. _____   leather   wool   plain   linen
   e. _____   rip   sleeveless   stain   too big

2. Look in your dictionary. Write the type of material next to each description.

Material Matters

a. ____linen____ This was the first woven material. Ancient people learned how to make thread from the blue-flowered flax plant and weave it into cloth. Today it is often used to make jackets and suits.

d. _____ This is the most important material in the world. It is used everywhere for all kinds of clothing and many other products. It comes from a plant that grows in hot climates.

b. _____ Very early, people learned how to make animal skins into this material. They rubbed the skins with fat to make them soft. Later they learned to use plants to soften the skins.

e. _____ This material is also used all over the world. It is made from the hair of an animal. It is soft, warm, and naturally waterproof!

c. _____ For thousands of years, only the Chinese knew how to make clothing from this beautiful material. Around 500 A.D., two men stole several eggs of the insects that make the thread. They took the eggs to the West, and the secret was out!

f. _____ This synthetic material comes from the laboratory, not from a plant or animal. It's used to make pantyhose and many other items of clothing.

3. Look at the pictures. Circle the correct words to complete the article.

SUITABLE DRESSING

Men's formal business suits never seem to change very much these days.

However, it took a long time for men to get to this basic piece of clothing.

Here's how it happened.

During the 1500s in Europe, fashionable men wanted to look fat. Their

pants, called pumpkin breeches, were (short)/ long and baggy / tight. They
                                a.   **b.**

wore short / long, light / heavy, sleeveless / long-sleeved jackets, and
      c.   **d.**   **e.**

they even stuffed their clothes with cereal and horsehair to look bigger!

In the 1700s, men preferred to look thinner and taller. The rich and stylish

wore their pants shorter / longer and very tight / baggy, and they wore
           f.   **g.**

shoes with low / high heels and big buckles. Jackets became longer / shorter
        h.   **i.**

and looser / tighter, and men wore fancy / plain shirts under them.
    j.   **k.**

After the French Revolution in 1789, it became dangerous to dress like the

rich. Instead, many men dressed like workers in long / short pants and loose
                          l.

jackets. This outfit was a lot like the modern suit, but the parts did not match.

The man in the picture, for example, is wearing striped / checked brown
                           m.

pants with a polka-dotted / paisley vest and a solid / plaid green jacket.
         n.   **o.**

Finally, at the end of the 1800s, it became stylish to match the pants,

jacket, and vest. As you can see, the traditional formal / casual three-piece
                          p.

business suit has not changed much since then.

4. What about you? How have styles changed in your country in the past 100 years? Write at least three sentences. Use your own paper.

Challenge Describe traditional clothing for men or women from a culture you know well. What materials, colors, and patterns do people wear? **Example:** *In Oman, women wear short tunics and long, baggy pants. The weather is very hot, so clothing is usually cotton or silk…*

Doing the Laundry

1. Look in your dictionary. **True** or **False**?

    a. A man is doing the laundry.   _____True_____

    b. He's at the dry cleaners.   _____

    c. The clothes in the laundry basket are ironed.   _____

    d. There's a clean shirt on the ironing board.   _____

    e. Someone hung a pair of jeans on the clothesline. _____

2. Circle the correct words to complete the laundry room instructions.

⦿ CLEANMACH INDUSTRIES, INC.

Washing Instructions

1. Pour (detergent) / spray starch into bottom of washer / dryer.
           a.   **b.**
2. Sort / Fold clothes and place loosely and evenly in the machine. DO NOT OVERLOAD.
    c.
3. Choose the correct temperature.
4. Close door. Hanger / Washer will not operate with door open.
               d.
5. Insert coin(s) into slot.
6. To add bleach / dryer sheets: Wait until laundry basket / washer has filled.
               e.   **f.**
DO NOT POUR directly onto clothes.
7. If you use fabric softener / detergent, add it when the rinse light goes on.
               g.

Drying Instructions

1. Clean the iron / lint trap before using the dryer.
            h.
2. Load / Unload the machine. DO NOT OVERLOAD. Overloading causes dirty / wrinkled clothes.
  i.   **j.**
3. Add dryer sheets / clothespins if you wish.
             k.
4. Close door. Dryer / Washer will not operate with door open.
              l.
5. Choose the correct temperature.
6. Insert coin(s) into slot. Push start button.
7. Remove dry / wet clothes immediately.
       m.

FOR SERVICE CALL (800) 555-3452

Challenge Look at some of your clothing labels. Write the laundry instructions.

1. Look in your dictionary. What can you use to…?

   a. repair a rip when you don't have needle and thread   _safety pin_

   b. cut material

   c. hold pins and needles

   d. remove threads from a hem or a seam

   e. measure your waist

   f. close the front of a windbreaker

   g. close the top of a dress (above the zipper)

   h. protect your finger when you sew

2. Look at the picture. Circle the correct words to complete the instructions.

Tailor Made

Please make these alterations:

Move the top button /(buttonhole.) It should be
               a.
below the collar / pocket.
       b.

Let out the collar / waistband.
        c.

Shorten / Lengthen the sleeves.
   d.

The right cuff / pocket is missing—please sew it on.
       e.

Let out / Take in the seams on the skirt and
     f.
hem / lengthen it so it's right at the knee.
  g.

3. What about you? Would you prefer to sew by hand or by machine? Why?

Challenge Design a piece of clothing. Draw it and write a description.

▶ **Go to page 174 for Another Look (Unit 5).**

The Body

1. Look in your dictionary. Match each pair with the connecting part.

___4___ **a.** hand / arm   **1.** elbow

_____ **b.** foot / calf   **2.** ankle

_____ **c.** calf / thigh   **3.** waist

_____ **d.** head / shoulders   **4.** wrist

_____ **e.** upper arm / lower arm   **5.** knee

_____ **f.** chest / abdomen   **6.** neck

2. Yoga is a very old form of exercise and meditation. Circle the correct words to complete the instructions.

PALMING   Rub your (palms) / gums together until your hands feel warm.
                              a.

Then hold them over your nose / eyes .
                             b.

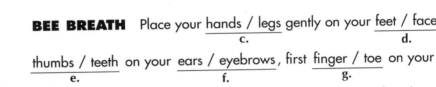

BEE BREATH   Place your hands / legs gently on your feet / face as follows:
                           c.   **d.**

thumbs / teeth on your ears / eyebrows , first finger / toe on your
    e.   **f.**   **g.**

eyelashes / toenails of your closed eyes, second on your chin / nose , third and
      h.   **i.**

fourth on your top and bottom lips / eyelids . When you breathe out, gently
                          j.

close your ears with your thumbs and put your tongue / bone against the
                                    k.

top of your throat / mouth to make a "zzzz" sound.
                  l.

THE BOW   Lie on your abdomen / artery . Reach back and hold your
                           m.

heels / ankles . Pull your thighs / hips and chest / buttocks off the floor.
  n.   **o.**   **p.**

Your skeleton / pelvis rests on the floor.
       q.

THE MOON   Kneel with your buttocks / rib cage on your arms / heels .
                      r.   **s.**

Put your hands / hair against your breast / back and hold your right
      t.   **u.**

wrist / vein . Bend forward until your chin / forehead touches the floor.
  v.   **w.**

3. Read the article. Label the foot with the matching parts of the body.

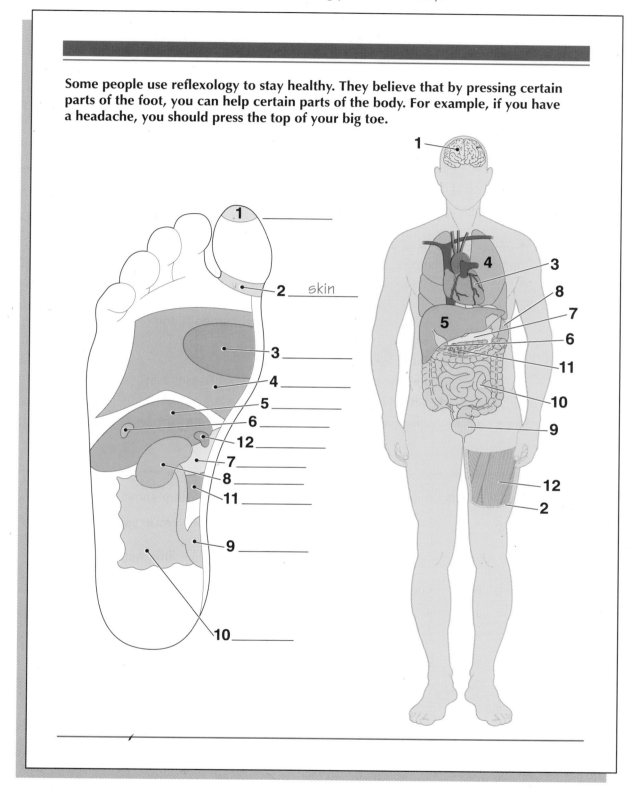

Some people use reflexology to stay healthy. They believe that by pressing certain parts of the foot, you can help certain parts of the body. For example, if you have a headache, you should press the top of your big toe.

1

1 _____

2 ___skin___

3 _____

4 _____

5 _____

6 _____

12 _____

7 _____

8 _____

11 _____

9 _____

10 _____

4 3
8
7
6
11
10
9
12
2
5

4. What about you? What do you do to relax and stay healthy? What parts of the body are these activities good for? Write at least five sentences. Use your own paper.

Challenge Write instructions for your favorite exercise.

Personal Hygiene

1. Look at the people in your dictionary. What is each person doing?

   a. "This air is really hot."   _drying her hair_

   b. "This cap really keeps my hair dry!"   _____

   c. "This mouthwash tastes great."   _____

   d. "I don't want to get a sunburn."   _____

   e. "I think all the shampoo is out of my hair now."   _____

   f. "Ouch! I cut my cheek."   _____

   g. "I don't use a brush when it's still wet."   _____

2. Number the steps in a manicure. Then write the item to use for each step. Look in your dictionary for help.

   ### FOUR STEPS TO BEAUTIFUL HANDS

   _____ a. When they are the right length, smooth and
               shape them.   _____

   __1__   b. First, take off the old polish.   _nail polish remover_

   _____ c. Finally, put the new color on your fingernails.   _____

   _____ d. After you remove it, cut your nails.   _____

3. Circle the correct words to complete the article.

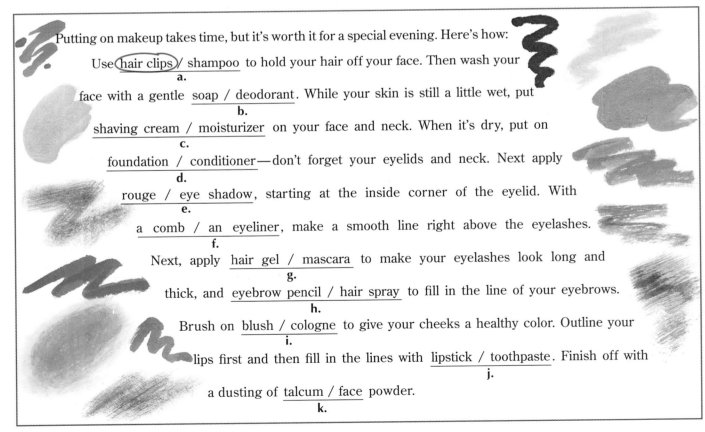

   Putting on makeup takes time, but it's worth it for a special evening. Here's how:

   Use (hair clips) / shampoo to hold your hair off your face. Then wash your
   a.

   face with a gentle soap / deodorant. While your skin is still a little wet, put
   b.

   shaving cream / moisturizer on your face and neck. When it's dry, put on
   c.

   foundation / conditioner—don't forget your eyelids and neck. Next apply
   d.

   rouge / eye shadow, starting at the inside corner of the eyelid. With
   e.

   a comb / an eyeliner, make a smooth line right above the eyelashes.
   f.

   Next, apply hair gel / mascara to make your eyelashes look long and
   g.

   thick, and eyebrow pencil / hair spray to fill in the line of your eyebrows.
   h.

   Brush on blush / cologne to give your cheeks a healthy color. Outline your
   i.

   lips first and then fill in the lines with lipstick / toothpaste. Finish off with
   j.

   a dusting of talcum / face powder.
   k.

4. Complete the crossword puzzle. Each clue is two words.

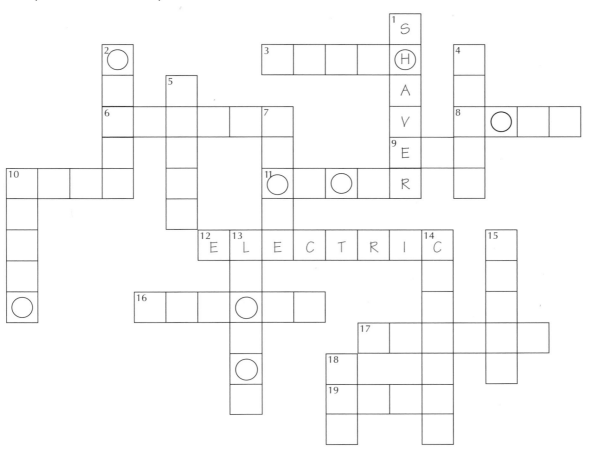

Clues

12 Across + 1 Down	You don't need water when you shave with it.
2 Down + 18 Down	It holds your hair in place.
3 Across + 10 Down	Use it after every meal.
5 Down + 6 Across	Be careful when you shave with them—they're sharp.
8 Across + 17 Across	Color your fingernails and toenails with it.
9 Across + 4 Down	It will make your eyes look bigger.
11 Across + 7 Down	Put it on your skin when you're finished shaving.
10 Across + 13 Down	It makes your skin feel smooth and soft.
14 Down + 19 Across	Style your hair with it.
16 Across + 15 Down	Remove food from between your teeth with it.

Now use the circled letters to answer this question:

What can you take to relax?   A __ __ __   __ __ __ __

5. What about you? What is your personal hygiene routine in the morning? List the steps. Use your own paper. Use Exercise 2 as a model.

Example: *First, I…*

Challenge Write detailed instructions for one of the following tasks:

washing and styling your hair   flossing and brushing your teeth   shaving

77

Symptoms and Injuries

1. Look in your dictionary. Which symptom or injury are they talking about?

   a. "This one in the back hurts."   <u>   toothache   </u>

   b. "The thermometer says 101."   _____

   c. "I ate too much ice cream."   _____

   d. "Next time I'll wear gloves when I rake the leaves."   _____

   e. "I need another blanket."   _____

   f. "Thanks for your handkerchief."   _____

2. Circle the correct words to complete the article.

Home Health Hints

Sick or injured? Try some of these tips:

- After a day in the sun, put oatmeal in your bathwater for a <u>swollen finger</u> / (<u>sunburn.</u>)
  a.

- A <u>sprained / cut</u> ankle or wrist is a common sports injury. Use RICE—Rest, Ice,
  b.
  Compression (wrapping in a tight elastic bandage), and Elevation (raising the injured part).

- Rub deodorant on <u>blisters / insect bites</u> caused by bees or spiders.
  c.

- Eating bad food can make you feel nauseous. You might even <u>vomit / faint</u>.
  d.
  Drinking warm cola can help you feel better.

- It's hard to swallow with a <u>backache / sore throat</u>. Soft ice cream helps the pain.
  e.

- Put an ice pack on a <u>rash / bruise</u> the first day. After 24 hours, use a heating pad.
  f.
  As it gets better, the area changes from blue, to red, to yellow.

- For <u>headaches / nasal congestion</u>, take hot baths and drink fluids to breathe more regularly.
  g.

- It's not bad to <u>cough / sneeze</u>—it gets bacteria out of your lungs. But an
  h.
  over-the-counter syrup helps you stop when you want to sleep.

Remember, these problems can be serious. If you feel very bad or if the problem continues or gets worse, see your doctor or other health professional.

3. What about you? What do you do when you have a(n)…?

SYMPTOM OR INJURY	REMEDY
stomachache	_____
earache	_____
rash	_____
Other: _____	_____

Challenge Find out about blisters. Write about how to prevent and treat them.

Illnesses and Medical Conditions

1. Look in your dictionary. Complete the chart.

Illness or Condition	What is it?	Contagious?	What are some symptoms?
a. asthma	a medical condition	No	tight feeling in chest, difficulty breathing; wheezing, coughing
b. _____	a common childhood illness	Yes	fever, blisters on face and body, and inside mouth, nose, or throat
c. _____	a very common infection of the nose, throat, etc.	Yes	nasal congestion or runny nose, sore throat, cough, low fever, tiredness, watering eyes
d. _____	a condition caused by the pancreas not making enough insulin	No	tiredness, thirst, increased hunger, and weight loss
e. _____	an infection most common in infants and children	No	nervousness, earache, "full" feeling in the ear, fever, difficulty hearing
f. _____	a common illness	Yes	chills, fever, muscle aches, cough, sore throat, runny nose, headache
g. _____	a condition often caused by hard and narrow arteries	No	(Often no symptoms in the beginning.) Later: chest pains, heart attack
h. _____	the virus that causes AIDS	Yes	swollen glands, sore throat, fever, skin rash
i. _____	a common childhood illness	Yes	fever, cough, red eyes, red rash on forehead and around ears, and, later, whole body
j. _____	a common childhood illness	Yes	swollen glands (between ear and jaw), fever, headache, sore throat
k. _____	a throat infection	Yes	fever, throat pain, headache, general sick feeling, ear pain, swollen glands in neck, bright red throat
l. _____	a lung disease	Yes	(Often no symptoms in the beginning.) Later: flu-like symptoms, low fever, loss of weight, tiredness, cough (with blood), chest pain, difficult breathing

Based on information from: Griffith, H. W.: *Complete Guide to Symptoms, Illness, and Surgery*, 3rd ed.
(NY: The Body Press/Perigee Books, 1995)

2. What about you? Check (✔) the illnesses or conditions you had as a child.

☐ measles   ☐ mumps   ☐ chicken pox   ☐ asthma

☐ allergy   ☐ Other: _____

Challenge Find out about high blood pressure. What is it? Is it contagious? What are some symptoms?

79

Health Care

1. Look in your dictionary. **True** or **False**? Correct the underlined words in the false sentences.

exercising

a. The couple in D is ~~taking medicine~~.   _____False_____

b. The man with a cane is in a <u>pharmacy</u>.   _____

c. The girl in E is getting <u>acupuncture</u>.   _____

d. The man in A is <u>getting bed rest</u>.   _____

e. The <u>audiologist</u> is putting eyeglasses on a girl.   _____

f. The <u>orthopedist</u> is putting on a cast.   _____

2. Which medicine are they talking about? Read the labels. Write the type of medicine after each statement. Use the words in the box.

capsules	cough syrup	ointment

CORTICARE

INDICATIONS:
Use on insect bites and rashes caused by poison ivy or poison oak.

DIRECTIONS:
Apply a small amount of Corticare 1 to 3 times a day.

WARNING: FOR EXTERNAL USE ONLY

ABC/pharmacy
RX:2596 Date filled:6/9/01
BLACK, RONALD
Take 1 three times a day with food. Finish entire prescription.
BEMOX 250 MG.
DR. SUSAN BROWN   Qty: 30

DRUGWORLD
RX:789 Date filled:1/1/97
CHARNOV, RUDY
Take 2 tsp. by mouth every 4 hours
POLYRISTINE CS
DR. PAUL RIME
Amount:120 ml. Exp.12/31/98
DO NOT **DRIVE** WHILE TAKING THIS MEDICATION

a. It's a liquid.   _____cough syrup_____

b. You can use this three times a day.   _____

c. The dosage is one, three times a day.   _____

d. This is an over-the-counter medication.   _____

e. Take this for ten days.   _____

f. The expiration date has already passed.   _____

g. Don't put this in your mouth!   _____

h. There's no warning label.   _____

i. Have some yogurt with this.   _____

j. This will make you feel sleepy.   _____

3. Circle the correct words to complete the diary entries.

Feb. 11—Woke up in the hospital with crutches /(casts) on both my legs! I can't
a.
remember anything about the accident. Jim's OK, thank goodness. He has
a sling / walker on his arm, but that's all. Here comes the nurse...
b.

Feb. 14— Jim visited me today and pushed me around the hospital in a
wheelchair / humidifier. He didn't come before because he had to
c.
use nasal spray / get bed rest for a few days, but he's fine now.
d.

March 24- They took off the casts / glasses and put on hearing aids / braces. Now
e.   f.
I can hold my air purifier / walker in front of me, and move around on my own.
g.
After a couple of weeks, I'll be ready for a pair of crutches / contact lenses.
h.

April 8- I can stand! I work with Carlos, my physical therapist / chiropractor,
i.
every day. I have to learn to use my legs again. The exercises hurt a lot. I put
an antacid / a heating pad on my painful muscles after therapy. At first I used
j.
pain relievers / throat lozenges, but I don't like to change my diet / take medicine.
k.   l.

April 25- Acupuncture / Immunization is helping! It's amazing! A needle in my
m.
shoulder makes my knees feel better. Now I use eye drops / prescription medication
n.
only when I really need it.

April 28—Tomorrow I go home! It's been more than two months! I still need to use
a cane / tablet, but Carlos says it won't be long now until I can walk without any help.
o.

4. What about you? What over-the-counter medicine do you have at home? Look at the labels and make a chart like the one below. Use your own paper.

Form	Dosage	Indications	Warning
tablets	1–2 tablets every 4–6 hours	to prevent nausea	Do not take if you have a breathing problem.

Challenge Write about an accident or illness that you or someone you know have recovered from. What were the treatments and medications? What were the steps to recovery?

1. Look in your dictionary. What happened? Write the medical condition.

a. The little girl in the laundry room _____*swallowed poison*_____ .

b. The woman in the snow _____ .

c. The man with the toaster _____ .

d. The boy in the doctor's office _____ .

e. The man pouring coffee _____ .

f. The girl under the blue blanket _____ .

g. The woman at the dinner table _____ .

2. Circle the correct words to complete the article.

How Safe Are You at Home?

Not very. As you probably know, most accidents occur at home. The chart below shows the number of people who were (injured) / unconscious in just one year using everyday products.
a.

Estimated number of injuries in the U.S.

Product	Estimated injuries
Stairs, steps	1,055,355
Bicycles	604,066
Knives	460,625
Bathtubs/showers	151,852
Drugs/medications	115,814
Razors/shavers	43,691
Hot water	43,457
TVs	36,457
Irons	16,447
Pesticides	16,281

Based on information from: Consumer Product Safety Commission (1993)

Falls are the number one cause of all household injuries. More than a million and a half people fell / had an allergic reaction while
b.
using stairs, steps, or bicycles. Some of the 151,852 injuries occurring in the bathtub or shower were also caused by falls.

How else are people getting hurt? In addition to falls, some people drowned / swallowed poison
c.
or burned themselves / got frostbite while
d.
bathing or showering. More than 500,000 people cut themselves and bled / couldn't breathe while
e.
using knives or razors, and over 100,000 people burned themselves / overdosed on drugs
f.
or got an electric shock / had an allergic reaction
g.
while taking medicine. ◆

3. What about you? How can you prevent some of the injuries in Exercise 2? Use your own paper.

Example: *To prevent frostbite, I wear gloves when it's very cold.*

Challenge Look at the chart in Exercise 2. How do you think people hurt themselves using TVs? irons? pesticides?

1. Look in your dictionary. Complete the information from a first-aid manual.

Always keep your medicine chest or first aid kit well supplied. Include:

a. _____*gauze*_____ for holding pads in place, or (if sterile) for covering cuts

b. _____ for removing pieces of glass or wood from the skin

c. _____ for preventing movement of a broken or sprained arm, finger, etc.

d. _____ for covering large cuts and burns

e. _____ for holding pads and gauze in place

f. _____ for preventing infection of cuts

g. _____ for covering small cuts

h. _____ for pouring on a new cut to help prevent infection

i. _____ for putting around a sprained ankle

j. _____ for treating rashes and allergic skin reactions

k. _____ for reducing pain and swelling

Note: A deep cut that continues to bleed may need _____ . Contact your doctor
                                                                          l.
or go to a clinic or hospital emergency room. People with special medical conditions such as diabetes,

heart disease, or serious allergies, should wear a _____ to identify the problem.
                                                                m.

2. Write the name of the lifesaving techniques. Use the words in the box.

CPR	~~Heimlich maneuver~~	rescue breathing

a. ___Heimlich maneuver___ Named after the doctor who invented it, this technique is used on people who are choking on food or another object.

b. _____ Performed mouth to mouth, this technique is used on people who have stopped breathing.

c. _____ This technique is used on people who have stopped breathing as a result of a heart attack, choking, or drowning. It involves mouth-to-mouth breathing and heart compression (massage) and should only be done by people with training.

3. What about you? Are there first-aid items that you use that are not in your dictionary? Write about them.

_____ for _____

Challenge Write the first-aid steps for a cut finger. (The finger is bleeding, but the cut is not deep.)

Clinics

1. Look at the medical clinic in your dictionary. What are the people talking about?

   a. "It was hard to read after the third line." _____ *eye chart*

   b. "According to <u>this</u>, your weight is 176." _____

   c. "Can you please fill <u>this</u> out for me?" _____

   d. "According to <u>this</u>, your pressure is fine." _____

   e. "Relax. <u>This</u> will only hurt a little." _____

   f. "According to <u>this</u>, you have a low fever." _____

   g. "When I listen through <u>this</u>, your lungs sound clear." _____

2. Complete the pamphlet. Use the words in the box.

cavities	braces	dentist	fillings	hygienist
	orthodontist	patients	~~tartar~~	

COMMON DENTAL QUESTIONS

Q: What is ____*tartar*____?
   a.

A: A hard substance that forms on your teeth.

Only a _____ or
   b.

dental _____
   c.

can remove it.

Q: I never get

_____.
   d.

Do I still need to

make appointments

every year?

A: Yes. Dentists also check for

other problems including gum disease and

cancer.

Q: My daughter just got _____ to
   e.

straighten her teeth. Am I too old for them?

A: No. Today more than one out of

four _____ visiting
   f.

the _____ is
   g.

an adult.

Q: I have a lot of old

silver and gold

_____. Is
   h.

there anything I can do about

their appearance?

A: They can be replaced by newer types that look

more like your own teeth.

Challenge Write two more questions about dental care like the ones in Exercise 2. Try to find the answers.

1. Look in your dictionary. What are the people doing?

a. "Open wide and say *ahh*." ___looking in his throat___

b. "Can the doctor see me in the morning?" _____

c. "Look straight at me." _____

d. "You don't have a fever." _____

e. "I'm getting all the tartar off." _____

f. "I'm almost finished. Then I'll fill it." _____

g. "You won't feel any pain after this." _____

2. Complete the pamphlet. Use the words in the box.

~~check your blood pressure~~	draw blood	examine your eyes
listen to your heart	look in your throat	take an X ray

• **Dr. Gregory Sarett** •

The Medical Exam—What to Expect

Dr. Sarett will check your height and weight. He will also ___check your blood pressure___
a.
to see if it is too high or too low. Then, using a stethoscope, he will _____
b.
while you are lying down and while you are sitting up. He will use

the stethoscope to listen to your lungs and abdomen, too. Then,

using an ophthalmoscope (an instrument with a light), he will

_____. If there is a problem, he may suggest you see an ophthalmologist.
c.

He will also _____, nose, and ears. The doctor may do other
d.
tests. He may, for example, _____ and send it to a lab for testing.
e.
He may _____ of your chest. At the end of the exam, he will discuss
f.
the results and make recommendations. You should feel free to ask him any questions before, during, or

after the exam.

3. What about you? How often do you go for a...?

a. medical checkup _____ b. dental checkup _____

Challenge Write a paragraph about what to expect during a dental exam.

A Hospital

1. Look in your dictionary. **True** or **False**? Correct the <u>underlined</u> words in the false sentences.

    a. The obstetrician's patient is wearing a ~~hospital gown~~. _dress_   _False_

    b. There's a <u>medical waste disposal</u> inside the patient's room.   _____

    c. The <u>bedpan</u> is next to the hospital bed.   _____

    d. The <u>X-ray</u> technician is drawing blood from the patient.   _____

    e. There's a glass on the <u>bed table</u>.   _____

    f. A volunteer is carrying <u>books</u> to a patient.   _____

    g. An RN is carrying <u>food</u>.   _____

    h. A licensed practical nurse is talking to the <u>dietitian</u>.   _____

    i. Two <u>orderlies</u> are taking a patient on a stretcher into the emergency room.   _____

    j. The <u>anesthesiologist</u> in the operating room is wearing a surgical cap.   _____

2. Circle the correct words to complete the information from a hospital pamphlet.

The Operation—What to Expect

In most cases, orderlies will take you to the <u>emergency</u> / (<u>operating</u>)
                                              a.

room on a <u>gurney</u> / <u>tray</u>. They will then carefully move you to the
          b.

<u>nurse's station</u> / <u>operating table</u>, where the surgery will take place.
             c.

Your surgical team (the anesthesiologist, surgical nurses, and, of

course, the <u>dietitian</u> / <u>surgeon</u>) will be there. In order to avoid
             d.

infection, they will wear surgical <u>caps</u> / <u>gloves</u> on their heads, and
                       e.

sterile latex <u>gloves</u> / <u>gowns</u> on their hands. All the instruments will be
            f.

sterilized, too. During the operation, the <u>anesthesiologist</u> / <u>volunteer</u>
                       g.

will monitor all your <u>medical charts</u> / <u>vital signs</u> (blood pressure,
             h.

breathing, and heart rate). An <u>IV</u> / <u>RN</u>, attached to a vein in your
            i.

arm, will provide you with fluids, and, if necessary, medication.

3. Write the full forms for these abbreviations.

    a. RN   ____*registered nurse*____   **c.** IV   _____

    b. EMT   _____   **d.** LVN _____

4. Look at the chart. Write the numbers to complete the sentences.

Doctors by Sex and Specialty in the United States		
SPECIALTY	**MALE**	**FEMALE**
anesthesiology	22,978	5,170
cardiology	15,563	915
internal medicine	67,138	18,701
obstetrics/gynecology	23,497	8,090
ophthalmology	14,691	1,742
pediatrics	23,842	16,573
psychiatry	27,377	9,028
radiology	7,064	784

Based on information from the American Medical Association, 1992

    a. There are ____1,742____ female eye doctors in the United States.

    b. The number of male eye doctors is _____.

    c. There are only _____ female doctors who are X-ray specialists.

    d. _____ male doctors are heart specialists.

    e. _____ male doctors specialize in mental illness (for example, serious sadness or nervousness).

    f. _____ female doctors specialize in women's health care.

    g. _____ men specialize in children's medicine.

5. What about you? Who would you prefer? Check (✔) the columns.

	MALE	FEMALE	NO PREFERENCE
a. internist			
b. cardiologists			
c. psychiatrists			
d. ophthalmologists			
e. orderlies			
f. obstetricians			
g. pediatricians			
h. nurses			

Challenge   Find out the names of other kinds of medical specialists. What do they do?

               Example: *An orthopedist is a bone doctor.*

▶ **Go to page 175 for Another Look (Unit 6).**

City Streets

1. Look in your dictionary. Where can you get…?

		PLACE	LOCATION
a.	a sandwich	coffee shop	Main and Elm
b.	a cake		
c.	a haircut		
d.	the best view of the city		
e.	traveler's checks		
f.	a carton of milk		
g.	oil for your car		
h.	a new couch		
i.	a used car		
j.	a hammer		
k.	a room for the night		

2. Complete the tourist information. Use the words in the box.

> city hall   hospital   hotel   library   office building
>
> park   post office   school   ~~skyscraper~~

PLACES OF INTEREST IN NEW YORK CITY

- **Empire State Building**   Over 1,250 feet tall, this building is

  the most famous _____skyscraper_____ in New York City.
  a.

  It opened in 1931 as an _____, and for
  b.

  many years it was the tallest building in the world.

- **Bellevue**   Opened in 1792, for the treatment of infectious diseases, this _____
  c.

  is one of the oldest and largest medical centers in the United States.

- **U.S. General** _____   Handling more than five million letters and packages
  d.

  a day, this is the largest mail processing center in the world. It is open 24 hours a day.

- **New York Public** _____ With over

  e.

  8,000,000 books in its 45 branches, this is the main building

  of the largest circulating system in the world. The main reading

  room seats 768 readers.

- _____ Built in 1803–1811, this is the center of New York City's government.

  f.

  The mayor's office is on the ground floor.

- **Waldorf-Astoria** This famous _____ has 1,852 guest rooms. The beautiful

  g.

  lobby is filled with business people and tourists from all over the world who stay here while visiting

  New York City.

- **Central** _____ This beautiful

  h.

  place of much-needed "green" is 2½ miles long and

  ½ mile wide. In addition to trees, flowers, gardens, and

  a lake, it contains a zoo, tennis courts, and a theater.

- **Cooper Union** Completed in 1859, this _____ is one of the oldest in the

  i.

  United States. Free classes were given day and night to fit working people's schedules. Students of

  all ages still study there today.

3. What about you? Would you want to live near a…? Check (✔) the boxes.

	YES	NO	WHY?
police station	☐	☐	_____
park	☐	☐	_____
fire station	☐	☐	_____
health club	☐	☐	_____
parking garage	☐	☐	_____
theater	☐	☐	_____
Other: _____	☐	☐	_____

Challenge Make a list of places for tourists to visit in your city or town. Include some information
about each place.

An Intersection

1. Look in your dictionary. Where can a shopper use these coupons?

a.

BARGAIN PAK COUPON

FREE

Burger, Fries, and
Medium Drink

When you buy a lunch
combo at the regular price.

fast food restaurant

d.

Manufacturer's Coupon

SAVE $1.50

When you buy two boxes of Nuts 'n Bran
or Apple Oatmeal Cereal

b.

Offer expires: 11/30

Brite Aid Coupon

½ PRICE
This Month Only

All _Brite Aid_
Children's Cold Medicines

e.

STORE COUPON

GLOSSIES

Free Roll of Film

with every processing order of
two rolls or more

c.

Bargain Pak Coupon

FALL SPECIAL

20% OFF

Winter Coats, Sweaters, Jackets
not valid after 11/30

f.

STORE COUPON

Buy 12
Get 1 FREE

(With a FREE cup of coffee)

Baked Fresh Daily!

2. Where can you hear…? Use your dictionary if you need help.

Dad: I can't read the menu.
Tim: Drive forward a little.

a. _drive-thru window_

Anne: How much change do I need?
Clerk: Two quarters for ten pages.

b. _____

Bob: Where's the bleach?
Kim: On top of the dryer.

c. _____

Pete: Do you get Spanish papers?
Owner: _El Diario_ comes on Tuesdays.

d. _____

3. Look at the picture. <u>Underline</u> eight more mistakes in the newspaper article.

Local News

Last week, Fran Bates rode her <u>motorcycle</u> into Mel Smith's car. There were no injuries. A customer entered the nail salon with a dog and was asked to leave. Two children opened the mailbox on Elm Street. Chief Dane closed it and called their parents. A shopper parked a car in the crosswalk on Main Street and received a parking ticket.

The town council met yesterday and voted to fix the streetlight at Main and Elm. Pedestrians say they cannot cross the street safely. Officer Dobbs reported that the parking meter on that corner should also be fixed. May Miller mentioned a problem outside her convenience store. She said the buses don't come often enough. Finally, the council voted for another drive-thru window. Shoppers have complained about long lines for the one in service.

4. Rewrite the article correctly. Use your own paper.

Example: *Last week Fran Bates rode her bicycle...*

<u>Challenge</u> Look at the picture in Exercise 3. Write about other problems.

91

A Mall

1. Look in your dictionary. Check (✔) the activities you can do at this mall. Write the kind of store you can do them in. (Do not use *department store*.)

☐	Buy cough syrup	_____
☑	Buy a birthday card	_card shop_
☐	Look at CD players	_____
☐	Get clothes dry-cleaned	_____
☐	Rent movies	_____
☐	Plan a vacation	_____
☐	Get new eyeglasses	_____
☐	Buy flowers	_____
☐	Buy a dictionary	_____
☐	Buy a dog	_____
☐	Mail letters	_____
☐	Buy chocolates	_____

2. Two teenagers are shopping at another mall. Look at the mall directory on page 93 of this book. Read the conversations and write the kind of place for each one.

a. **Server:** What flavor?

    Bee: Strawberry, please.

                                               ice cream stand

b. **Amy:** What do you think? Too curly?

    Bee: No. It's a terrific perm.

c. **Amy:** I love that new song by Kicking Pumpkins.

    Bee: Let's go buy the CD.

d. **Bee:** Hey! That's Jim coming down.

    Amy: Let's meet him at the bottom.

e. **Bee:** Let's go here for your high heels.

    Amy: Good idea. I usually don't like what they have at Crane's.

f. **Amy:** Do you like these earrings?

    Bee: Yeah. You look good in gold.

g. **Bee:** What do you want to eat? We have three choices.

    Amy: I think I'd like Mexican food.

h. **Amy:** Excuse me. Where's the main entrance?

    Clerk: Right behind you.

3. Look at Exercise 2. Circle the numbers and symbols on the map and draw Amy and Bee's route.

4. What about you? Is there a mall near your home? Imagine that you're going there this weekend. What stores will you go to? What will you do there? (If there isn't a mall nearby, you can use the one in your dictionary.)

Example: *I'll go to the toy store and buy some puzzles for my niece.*

Challenge Where would you prefer to shop, downtown (the business center of a town or city) or at a shopping mall? Think about weather conditions, the transportation you can use to get there, the kinds of shops, prices, and entertainment. Write at least five sentences.

A Childcare Center

1. Look at the childcare center in your dictionary. Correct the underlined words in these false sentences.

   stroller
   a. A little boy is sitting in a ~~carriage~~.

   b. A <u>childcare worker</u> is dropping off her daughter.

   c. The children's clothes are <u>on the floor</u>.

   d. A childcare worker is sitting in a <u>high chair</u> and looking at a picture book.

   e. Another worker is changing a baby's diaper <u>in a playpen</u>.

2. Circle the correct words to complete the instructions to childcare workers.

KidCo
                                                    October 4

Don't (feed) / dress Stefan or give him a diaper pin / bottle after 2:20 p.m.
      a.   **b.**

His mother wants to <u>nurse / play with</u> him when she comes at 5:30.
                       c.

Peter's first day at KidCo! His father will <u>drop him off / pick him up</u> at
                                          d.

7:30 a.m. If he cries when his father leaves, <u>rock him / tie his shoes</u> and
                                                      e.

<u>read him a story / play with him</u>. His favorite book is "The Cat in the Hat."
                  f.

Rachel has an ear infection. Please <u>change her diapers / pick her up</u> and
                                              g.

hold her whenever she cries. Call her mother if she has a fever.

Steven <u>tells a story / takes a nap</u> from 11:00 to noon. When he wakes up,
               h.

<u>drop off / feed him</u> his lunch and then let him play in the <u>playpen / baby food</u>.
   i.   **j.**

Tracy gets a rash from <u>wipes / walkers</u> and <u>carriages / disposable diapers</u>. When
                            k.   **l.**

you <u>tell her a story / change her diapers</u>, please use a washcloth and cloth diapers.
                 m.

César just started to <u>dress / rock</u> himself and <u>tie / hold</u> his shoes!
                             n.   **o.**

He needs extra time to get ready before he goes outside to play.

3. Cross out the word that doesn't belong. Give a reason.

a. high chair ~~baby backpack~~ potty seat

   Babies don't sit on a backpack.

b. pacifier bib diaper

_____

c. formula baby food disinfectant

_____

d. diaper pail rattles toys

_____

e. carriage stroller teething ring

_____

4. Complete these thank you notes. Use the words in the box.

baby carrier	bib	car safety seat	~~high chair~~	playpen

a.
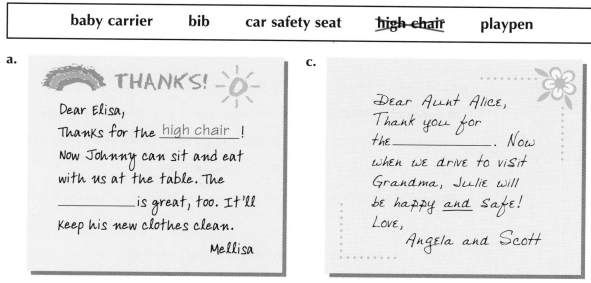
THANKS!

Dear Elisa,
Thanks for the _high chair_ !
Now Johnny can sit and eat
with us at the table. The
_____ is great, too. It'll
keep his new clothes clean.

Mellisa

c.
Dear Aunt Alice,
Thank you for
the _____. Now
when we drive to visit
Grandma, Julie will
be happy _and_ safe!
Love,
    Angela and Scott

b.
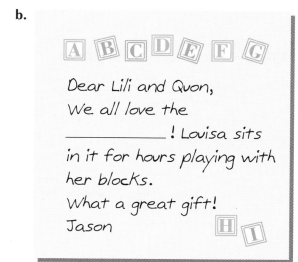
A B C D E F G

Dear Lili and Quon,
We all love the
_____ ! Louisa sits
in it for hours playing with
her blocks.
What a great gift!
Jason
H I

d.
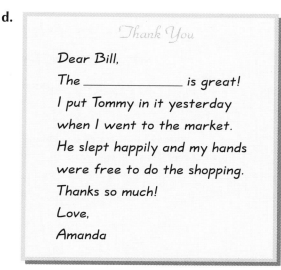
Thank You

Dear Bill,
The _____ is great!
I put Tommy in it yesterday
when I went to the market.
He slept happily and my hands
were free to do the shopping.
Thanks so much!
Love,
Amanda

Challenge Look in your dictionary. Choose a baby gift for someone you know. Explain your choice.

U.S. Mail

1. Look in your dictionary. What are the people talking about?

   a. "That's not enough. You need to put another <u>one</u> on."   <u>   stamp   </u>

   b. "<u>She</u> usually comes around 11:30."   <u>   </u>

   c. "<u>It</u> says May 7th."   <u>   </u>

   d. "Open <u>it</u>! It could be the vase we ordered."   <u>   </u>

2. Circle the correct words to complete the information about the U.S. postal services.

(**Letter**)/ **Package:** First-class mail weighing 13 oz. or less.
        a.
Rate: First oz. $.33, each additional oz. $.22.

Postcard / Postmark: $.20
       b.

Priority Mail: First-class mail weighing more than 13 oz. Sample rates: Up to 2 lbs.

$3.20; 2–3 lbs. $4.30; 3–4 lbs. $5.40.

Express / Certified Mail: The fastest way to send a letter or package. The post
       c.
office guarantees to <u>deliver / receive</u> it overnight—365 days a year including weekends.
         d.
Sample rates: Up to 8 oz. $10.75; 8 oz.–2lbs. $15.00.

Parcel Post: For <u>letters / packages</u> weighing 1 lb. or more. Rate depends on weight
         e.
and distance.

Certified / Priority Mail: When you <u>address / send</u> important mail, you can get a
    f.   **g.**
mailing receipt. The receiver's post office also keeps a record. Rate: $1.40 plus first-class

or priority <u>postmark / postage</u>.
         h.

Aerogrammes / Overnight Mail: Air letter sheets that you fold and close to form
         i.
<u>an envelope / a postcard</u>. Rate: All countries $.50.
      j.

Note: Rates can change. Check your local post office.

3. What about you? What kinds of mail service do you use? How much do they cost?

<u>   </u>

Challenge You're in Florida. Use the information in Exercise 2 to figure out the postage for....

      a. an aerogramme to Japan   <u>   </u>   **c.** a 14-oz. letter to Texas   <u>   </u>

      b. a 3-oz. letter to New York   <u>   </u>   **d.** a postcard to Michigan   <u>   </u>

1. Look in your dictionary. Complete the sentences.

   a. The _____teller_____ is helping a customer.

   b. The _____ is wearing a uniform.

   c. Rita Rose keeps her jewelry in a _____ in the bank's _____.

   d. The customer at the ATM machine is using a _____ number.

2. Look at the monthly statement. Complete the sentences. Use the words in the box.

deposit	~~checking account~~	balance	savings account
ATM card	withdrew	transferred	deposit slip

Monthly Statement

March 31–April 30, 2002

Jamal Al-Marafi   Account Number: 0125-00

Opening Balance
$1,117.20

Date	Transaction	Amount	Balance
3/31/02	Quikcash ATM #123	50.00	1,067.20
4/01/02	Deposit	1,283.47	2,350.67
4/20/02	Transfer to Checking	850.00	1,500.67
4/29/02	Withdrawal	100.00	1,400.67

Account Number: 0135-08

Opening Balance
$849.00

Date	Transaction	Amount	Balance
4/05/02	Check #431	732.00	117.00
4/11/02	Quikcash ATM #123	75.00	42.00
4/20/02	Transfer from Savings	850.00	892.00

   a. Jamal's _checking account_ number is 0135-08.

   b. His _____ number is 0125-00.

   c. On April 11, Jamal used his _____ to get cash.

   d. When Jamal got his $1,283.47 paycheck, he made a _____.

   e. He used a _____ for his April 1 transaction.

   f. On March 31, the _____ in Jamal's checking account was $849.00.

   g. On April 29, Jamal _____ $100.00.

   h. He _____ $850.00 from savings to checking on April 20.

Challenge Find out about a local bank. Which services are free? Which ones have fees? How much are they?

A Library

1. Look in your dictionary. What do the <u>underlined</u> words refer to?

    a. You can look up the Nile River in <u>this book</u>. _____*atlas*_____ or _____

    b. <u>It</u> has a lot of small drawers. _____

    c. You'll need <u>it</u> to check out your book. _____

    d. The library clerk is <u>there</u>. _____

2. Complete the reference librarian's answers. Use your dictionary for help.

Patron: Do you have the movie *Romancing the Stone*?

Librarian: Yes. The ____*videocassettes*____ are right there.
                                   a.

Patron: I'm looking for a job. Do you have this weekend's job ads?

Librarian: The Sunday _____ is in the _____ section.
                                         b.   **c.**

Patron: Where can I find information about fashion and makeup?

Librarian: We get several fashion _____ every month. Try those.
                                           d.

Patron: In 1990 the *Gazette* had an article about our city. I'd like to read it.

Librarian: We have the *Gazette* on _____ from 1890 to 1997. You can
                                           e.

    read it on the _____.
                   f.

Patron: Do you have audiocassettes by The What? I love their music.

Librarian: No, but we have their new _____. It's next to the records.
                                          g.

Patron: I'm doing a report on Ghandi, but I don't know anything about him.

Librarian: You should read an article in an _____ first.
                                          h.

Patron: I'm looking for Grisham's new book. I don't remember what it's called.

Librarian: You don't need to know the _____. Just type the author's name
                                          i.

    into the _____ and press *Enter*.
               j.

Challenge   What items does your library have? Make a chart like the one below.

ITEM	EXAMPLE	CAN CHECK IT OUT?	HOW LONG?
book	*The Runaway Jury, by John Grisham*	yes	two weeks

1. Look in your dictionary. Who is…?

   a. wearing handcuffs   *the suspect*

   b. pointing to the defendant   _____

   c. typing   _____

   d. sitting next to the defense attorney in court   _____

   e. sitting in jail   _____

   f. standing in a corner in the courtroom   _____

2. Circle the correct words to complete the interview with a former convict.

INTERVIEW

PS Magazine: Dan Long, you've received awards for your work with young people. But you yourself ~~went to prison~~ / *stood trial for several years.*
            a.

Dan Long: Yes—for burglary. I was <u>released / arrested</u> three years ago. It
                              b.
was the happiest day of my life.

PS: Tell us about your experience with the legal system. You didn't have a job. How did you <u>hire a lawyer / stand trial</u>?
                                  c.

DL: I didn't. The court gave me one. And she was good. In fact, when we <u>gave the verdict / appeared in court</u>, she got the <u>guard / judge</u> to lower the
                      d.   **e.**
bail to $1,000.

PS: So what happened when you <u>sentenced the defendant / stood trial</u>?
                                        f.

DL: She did her best, but the <u>prosecuting / defense</u> attorney had a lot of
                               g.
evidence against me.

PS: Were you surprised when the <u>police officer / jury</u> *gave the verdict?*
                                   h.

DL: No, but I was when the judge <u>sentenced / released</u> me. Seven years!
                                 i.
Now I tell young people what it's like to spend years in <u>jail / court</u>.
                                          j.

Challenge   Write the story of the man in the dictionary who was arrested.

Crime

1. Look in your dictionary. Put each crime in the correct category.

CRIMES AGAINST PEOPLE	CRIMES AGAINST PROPERTY (BUILDINGS, CARS, ETC.)	SUBSTANCE ABUSE CRIMES (DRUGS AND ALCOHOL)
gang violence		

2. Look at the line graph. Complete the sentences. Use the words in the box. (You will use two words more than once.)

assaults	burglaries	murders	vandalism

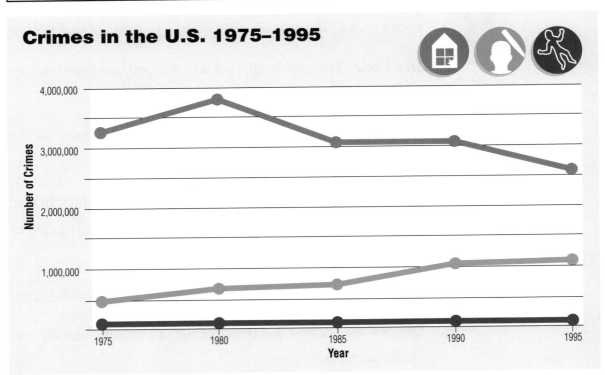

Crimes in the U.S. 1975–1995

Based on information from *FBI Uniform Crime Reports*

a. In 1990, there were about a million _____assaults_____ in the United States.

b. In 1990, there were about three million _____.

c. Between 1990 and 1995, the number of _____ went down.

d. The number of _____ has changed less than the other crimes.

e. The number of _____ went up between 1975 and 1995.

f. The chart does not have information about _____.

Challenge Look at **page 184** in this book. Complete the chart.

1. Look in your dictionary. Complete the newsletter with the correct advice.

Safety Tips

a. _____ Lock your doors.

A dead-bolt lock is your best protection. Door chains are also good.

b. _____

If you're at a party or a bar, choose a "designated driver."

c. _____

Always ask, "Who's there?" If you don't know them, don't let them in!

d. _____

It's easy for a criminal to grab something that is just hanging from your arm or shoulder.

e. _____

For men, the best place is an *inside* jacket pocket. For women, a *closed* purse.

f. _____

There's safety in numbers. Muggers usually look for *easy* victims.

g. _____

Remember: criminals don't want witnesses, so lights are your friends. Also, this way *you* can see who's on the street, and you won't be surprised!

h. _____

If you witness a crime or become a crime victim, dial 911 immediately!

The East Village Neighborhood Watch—Looking Out for You!

2. Look at the picture. What safety mistakes is the man making? Use the information in Exercise 1.

a. He isn't staying on well-lit streets.

b. _____

c. _____

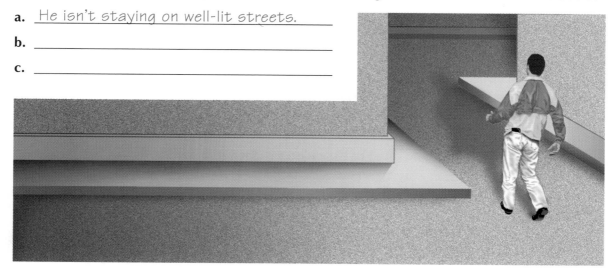

3. What about you? Which of the safety tips in Exercise 1 do you follow? Make a list. Use your own paper.

Challenge Interview five people. Find out about the safety tips they follow.

Emergencies and Natural Disasters

1. Look in your dictionary. Which disaster is the news reporter talking about?

a. "The same mountain erupted five years ago." *volcanic eruption*

b. "All homes near the beach were destroyed by the water." _____

c. "The two vehicles were badly damaged, but luckily, the drivers were not hurt in the crash at the intersection of Tenth and Elm." _____

d. "Store detectives found the little girl sitting on the floor." _____

e. "The twister destroyed several farms in its path." _____

2. Complete the newspaper articles. Use the words in the box.

| airplane crash | blizzard | drought | ~~earthquake~~ | explosion |
| fire | firefighters | hurricane | search and rescue team |

a.

Disaster Strikes Kobe, Japan

TOKYO, Jan. 17—An ____*earthquake*____ measuring 7.1 on the Richter scale hit the city of Kobe, Japan, killing more than 5,000 people and injuring 26,500 others. More than 100,000 buildings were destroyed.

b.

KILLS 109

MIAMI, May 11—A DC-9 jet en route to Atlanta went down in the Florida Everglades just a few minutes after takeoff from Miami. All 109 passengers were killed. The cause of the disaster is not yet known.

c.

INFERNO IN LONDON UNDERGROUND

LONDON, Nov. 17—Thirty died and 21 were seriously injured in a _____ in one of the busiest subway stations in the world. "As soon as I got on the escalator, I could smell burning," said one witness. Seconds later she saw the red flames and dark smoke. _____ rushed to the scene.

d.

BOMB _____ IN OKLAHOMA CITY KILLS 170

OKLAHOMA CITY, Apr. 19—A car bomb went off outside a federal office building killing 169 people. A member of the _____ also died while trying to save the victims. The bomb destroyed most of the nine-story building and damaged many other buildings in the area.

e.

High Winds in Jamaica

KINGSTON, Sept. 18— _____ Gilbert, the most powerful Atlantic storm ever recorded, struck the island of Jamaica and Mexico's Yucatan Peninsula leaving more than 200 dead. Winds reached 218 miles an hour. Whole trees flew through the air.

f.

THE _____ OF '93

BOSTON, Mar. 22—Described as a "hurricane with snow," the giant storm hit the eastern third of the United States. The winds created snow drifts as high as 14 feet in New England.

g.

A Long Dry Winter

SANTA BARBARA, March 23—As a result of 73% less rain than usual over the last year, California is experiencing its worst _____ since the 1930s. The state is going to stop water deliveries to farms in an effort to save water.

_____ **Challenge** Write a paragraph about an emergency or a natural disaster.

▶ **Go to page 176 for Another Look (Unit 7).**

Public Transportation

1. Look in your dictionary. What are they talking about? Where are they?

a. "It goes in this way." _____fare card_____ _____subway_____

b. "This says there's one at 3:02." _____ _____

c. "Use this to change at Avenue A." _____ _____

d. "It says $3.50 so I'll tip 50¢." _____ _____

2. Circle the correct words to complete the letter.

Dear Gray,

   I'm glad you decided to visit us in Plum Island. You can get here by public transportation, but take a book with you—it's a long trip!

   First, take a (bus) / taxi to Wyckoff Street. It's fast, and the meter / fare is only 75¢.
        a.   **b.**
I think one leaves every half hour. Check the schedule / route when you get to the
                                                          c.
track / bus stop. When you get off at Wyckoff, go down the stairs to the ferry / subway and
   d.   **e.**
buy a token / transfer. Take the WW or the Y train to Central Station. The Y only stops
       f.
there at certain hours. Check with the conductor / meter before you get on. At the
                                                    g.
taxi stand / train station, buy a round-trip fare card / ticket to Harbor Point. It costs $45.00
        h.   **i.**
and it takes about three hours. Sit in the front of the train / ferry or you'll get off in
                                                              j.
somebody's garden. The track / platform at Harbor Point is only a few yards long. There's a
                          k.
taxi stand / subway station across the route / tracks from the station. Tell the driver / passenger
        l.   **m.**   **n.**
you're taking the ferry / subway to Plum Island. They don't use meters / schedules,
                      o.   **p.**
but it costs $5.00. See you soon!

                                                          Enrico

3. What about you? What kinds of public transportation do you use? Make a chart. Use your own paper.

Example:

TYPE	FARE	HOW DO YOU PAY?	WHERE DO YOU GO?
ferry	$ .80 round trip	fare card	from home to work

Challenge Describe some advantages and disadvantages of public transportation.

1. Look in your dictionary. Where are they going?

    a. "Turn right here."   _around the corner_

    b. "This is our exit."   _____

    c. "Park Avenue and Third Street, please."   _____

    d. "Why don't they have an escalator?"   _____

2. Look at the map of Toronto. Circle the correct words to complete the directions.

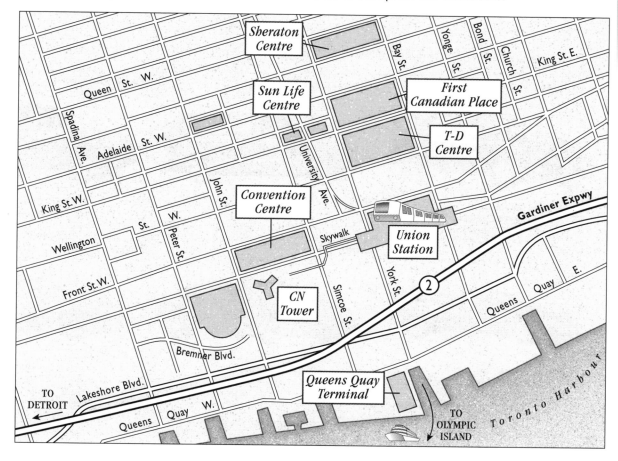

    a. To go from Union Station to Toronto Harbour, get off / (go under) the expressway on York Street.

    b. To go from the Convention Centre to the Sun Life Centre, get into / out of the taxi on King Street.

    c. To go from Queen's Quay Terminal to Olympic Island, go across / around Toronto Harbour.

    d. To go from Union Station to Detroit, get onto / off the expressway at York Street.

    e. To go from CN Tower to Union Station on foot, go over / under the Skywalk.

Challenge Write directions from your home to: school   the bus station   Other: _____

Cars and Trucks

1. Look in your dictionary. Read these ads. Write the kind of car or truck for sale.

a.
used to remove cars from the highway

tow truck

b.
great small-family car, blue exterior

_____

c.
16 wheels, 85-in. orange cab

_____

d.
bike rack, sleeps 4

_____

e.
yellow with black interior, small rip in top

_____

f.
beautiful green town car

_____

2. Look at the cars and answer the questions. (Do not write the make and model.)

Venus XL
6 passengers
20 miles/gallon
42" front legroom

Eton Grand Tour
7 passengers
20 miles/gallon
41.2" front legroom

Sol Aventura
6 passengers
17 miles/gallon
44" front legroom

Marvette
2 passengers
23 miles/gallon
42" front legroom

Land Ville
4 passengers
44 miles/gallon
42.5" front legroom

Dayton LaRey
5 passengers
23 miles/gallon
43.5" front legroom

Which…

a. uses the most gas? _____SUV_____

b. carries the fewest passengers? _____

c. is best for a big family? _____

d. has the least legroom? _____

e. is cheapest to drive? _____

f. carry the same number of passengers? _____ and _____

3. What about you? Look in your dictionary. Which car would you choose? Why? Use your own paper.

Example: _I would choose a pickup. I carry a lot of things, but not many passengers._

Challenge Look at newspaper ads. Find the price range of the car you chose in Exercise 3.

1. Look at **pages 88 and 89** in your dictionary. Begin at the southeast corner of Main and Elm streets. Follow the directions below. Where are you?

   a. Go one block north.   Elm and First

   b. Then go one block east. Turn left. Go straight for one block.   _____

   c. Then go one block east. Turn right. Go two blocks south.   _____

   d. Then go west for two blocks.   _____

2. Complete the written part of a test for a driver's license. Circle the letters of the correct answers.

   1. When you see a STOP sign, you must _____.
      a. go more slowly
      b. come to a complete stop
      c. turn right

   2. When you see this sign, you _____.
      a. must drive exactly 55 mph
      b. can drive 45 mph
      c. can drive 60 mph

   3. This sign means _____ crossing.
      a. pedestrian
      b. railroad
      c. school

   4. A DEAD END sign means _____.
      a. you can't enter the street
      b. the street is very dangerous
      c. the street ends

   5. This sign means you should look for _____.
      a. rest rooms
      b. rivers
      c. trains

   6. When you see this sign, you can make a _____.
      a. left turn
      b. right turn
      c. U-turn

   7. This sign indicates _____.
      a. handicapped parking
      b. a hospital
      c. no parking any time

Challenge Draw some other traffic signs. Explain their meanings.

Parts of a Car and Car Maintenance

1. Look in your dictionary. How many ... does the red car have?

a. hubcaps   _4_   e. gauges   _____

b. sideview mirrors   _____   f. rearview mirrors   _____

c. license plates   _____   g. windshield wipers   _____

d. jacks   _____   h. spare tires   _____

2. Complete the conversations. Use the words in the box.

accelerator	air conditioning	front seat	~~gas gauge~~	glove compartment
license plate	radio	rearview mirror	stick shift	temperature gauge

a. **Passenger:** Look, the _____ gas gauge _____ is almost on empty.

    Driver: There's a gas station. I'll stop there.

b. **Driver:** Where would you like to sit?

    Passenger: In the _____, next to you.

c. **Driver:** It would be nice to hear a traffic report.

    Passenger: I'll turn on the _____.

d. **Passenger:** It's getting hot in here.

    Driver: We can turn on the _____.

e. **Passenger:** Do we have a map?

    Driver: There should be one in the _____.

f. **Passenger:** That truck is getting very close!

    Driver: That's OK. I'm watching it in the _____.

g. **Passenger:** Step on the _____. You're going much too slow.

    Driver: OK.

h. **Passenger:** Look at the _____.

    Driver: Oh. The radiator needs coolant.

i. **Passenger:** That car is leaving the accident scene!

    Driver: Quick! Write down the _____ number!

j. **Passenger:** Do you like using a _____?

    Driver: Yes. I've always driven a car with a standard transmission.

3. Circle the correct words to complete information from a driver's manual.

Basic Driving

- The bumper / (steering wheel) gives you control over your car.
  a.
- Always have the correct amount of air in your hubcaps / tires. Check the pressure.
  b.
- When you step on your brake pedal / clutch, your car should stop quickly and smoothly.
  c.
- Jumper cables / Turn signals tell other drivers which direction you are going to go.
  d.
- Brake lights / Taillights tell other drivers that you are slowing or stopping.
  e.
- Your hood / horn lets other drivers and pedestrians hear that you are there.
  f.
- Lug wrenches / Headlights are important in night driving, rainy weather, and in fog.
  g.
- The heater / windshield should be free of cracks and breaks. Use your
  h.
  gear shift / windshield wipers to clean it.
  i.

Preventing Injuries

- Check your odometer / speedometer to see how fast you are going.
  j.
- New cars come with air bags / spare tires that open in case of an accident.
  k.
  They keep you from hitting your head against the dashboard / trunk or steering wheel.
  l.
- Back seats / Seat belts and shoulder harnesses help prevent injury or death in case of
  m.
  an accident. Always use them.
- Use your door jacks / locks to keep your doors from opening in an accident.
  n.

Air and Noise Pollution Control

- When your car needs fuel, get low-lead or lead-free gas / coolant. It pollutes less.
  o.
- Keep your engine / cigarette lighter in good condition with regular maintenance.
  p.
- Make sure there is enough coolant in the battery / radiator.
  q.
- Change the air / oil and filter regularly.
  r.
- If your car is making a lot of noise, you may need to replace your ignition / muffler.
  s.

Challenge Look at **page 184** in this book. Follow the instructions.

An Airport

1. Look in your dictionary. Who's speaking? About what?

a. "My other bag isn't on it!" _____passenger_____ _____carousel_____

b. "Number 24 is to your right." _____ _____

c. "You didn't sign it." _____ _____

d. "Put it over your face." _____ _____

2. Circle the correct words to complete the travel tips.

ESL International Travel Tips

Before Your Flight

★ Arrive at <u>customs</u>/(the airline terminal) at least two hours before your flight.
  a.

★ Check the <u>departure monitor</u>/<u>control tower</u> for information about your flight.
  b.

★ After going through security, go to the <u>check-in counter</u>/<u>baggage claim area</u>.
  c.

  Show your ticket to the <u>pilot</u>/<u>airline representative</u>.
  d.

★ Go to your <u>gate</u>/<u>carousel</u>.
  e.

★ Wait in the <u>cockpit</u>/<u>boarding area</u>.
  f.

On the Plane

★ Put your carry-on bags in the <u>luggage carrier</u>/<u>overhead compartment</u>.
  g.

★ Pay attention as your <u>airline representative</u>/<u>flight attendant</u> shows you how to
  h.

  put on your <u>oxygen mask</u>/<u>helicopter</u> and gives you other safety information.
  i.

★ Keep your <u>seat belt</u>/<u>tray table</u> fastened around your waist in case of turbulence.
  j.

★ Fill out <u>a declaration form</u>/<u>an arrival monitor</u> before you land.
  k.

After You Land

★ Go to the <u>check-in counter</u>/<u>baggage claim area</u> to get your luggage from the
  l.

  <u>luggage carrier</u>/<u>carousel</u>.
  m.

★ Take your bags through <u>customs</u>/<u>the boarding area</u>.
  n.

Have an enjoyable trip, and thanks for flying ESL Airlines!

Challenge Find out about a job in an airport. Would you like this job? Why or why not? Write a paragraph.

1. Look in your dictionary. **Before** or **After**? Circle the correct word.

   a. The passenger went through security before / (after) he checked his bags.

   b. He fastened his seat belt before / after he looked for the emergency exit.

   c. He requested a blanket before / after they experienced turbulence.

2. Look at the flight information. **True** or **False**? Write a question mark (**?**) if the information isn't there.

```
          ✈  HAPPY TRAVELS  ✈

ORTIZ/VILMA          PAGE 1 OF 1 FILE #142-34-02-54-2
        RECONFIRM RESERVATIONS 72 HRS PRIOR TO EACH FLIGHT. FAILURE TO DO SO MAY RESULT
            IN MISSING YOUR FLIGHT OR HAVING THE SPACE CANCELED BY THE AIRLINE.

    AIRWAY AIRLINES           FLIGHT  613     10MAR  SUN
    DEPART      0755A         NEW YORK LGA            CHECK-IN REQUIRED
    ARRIVE      1048A         MIAMI MIA               MEALS: SNACK

    AIRWAY AIRLINES           FLIGHT  695     10MAR  SUN
    DEPART      1115A         MIAMI MIA               SEAT 23D NON-SMOKING
    ARRIVE      0155P         SAN JUAN SJU            MEALS: SPECIAL LOW-SALT
```

   a. The passenger bought her ticket from Happy Travels.   True

   b. This is a boarding pass.   _____

   c. Her destination is New York.   _____

   d. The arrival time in Miami is 11:15 A.M.   _____

   e. The departure time from New York is 7:55 A.M.   _____

   f. Passengers will board flight 613 at 7:35 A.M.   _____

   g. Passengers can have two carry-on bags.   _____

   h. Flight 613 takes off Sunday morning.   _____

   i. It lands on Sunday afternoon.   _____

   j. There's a stopover of about 30 minutes.   _____

   k. The passenger has to change planes in San Juan.   _____

   l. She doesn't have to check in for flight 613.   _____

   m. She is in seat 23D on flight 695.   _____

   n. The seat is next to an emergency exit.   _____

   o. The passenger requested a special meal.   _____

   p. Passengers will claim their baggage at carousel 4.   _____

Challenge   Write a paragraph about a plane trip you (or someone you know) took.

▶ **Go to page 177 for Another Look (Unit 8).**

Types of Schools

1. Look in your dictionary. Read the teachers' comments and write the type of school the student is attending.

   a. Carrying that heavy book paid off. Good luck in college. _____high school_____

   b. You'll be a great mechanic, Marcia. _____

   c. Your English has improved a lot this semester, Ms. Rivera. _____

   d. José enjoys playing with blocks. _____

2. Complete the school directory. You can use your dictionary for help.

Name and Type of School	Public/Private/Parochial
a. Baychester _____High School_____ (Grades 9–12) 966 students • free	_____public_____
b. Berg County _____ (Continuing Education) ESL, Citizenship classes • 147 students • free	_____
c. Country Day _____ (Ages 3–5) 874 students • $6,000/yr.	_____
d. EMI _____ (Computer Training) 235 students • $670 per semester	_____
e. Gale _____ (Undergraduate, Graduate) 8,230 students • $6,000 per semester	_____
f. Hartwood _____ (Grades 1–5) 830 students • free	_____
g. St. Mary's _____ (Grades 6–8) 267 students • $1,125/yr.	_____

3. Write the letter of the school from Exercise 2 that each person attends.

   a. Our 13-year-old son needs small classes, but we can't pay much. _____a_____

   b. I work in a fast food restaurant during the day, and I get job training at night. _____

   c. I graduated from college in my country. I study English at night. _____

   d. My granddaughter is only four. She loves going to school. _____

   e. We have two children in elementary school. Our taxes pay for their education. _____

   f. I plan to go to law school after I graduate. _____

4. What about you? What types of schools did you attend for each level? What did you like or dislike about them? Write sentences. Use your own paper.

   Example: *I attended a public preschool. I liked it because we went on a lot of trips.*

Challenge Look at the pie chart on **page 184** in this book. Answer the questions.

1. Look in your dictionary. Write the dates.

    a. The student got feedback from another student.   <u>   Oct. 1   </u>

    b. The teacher gave a writing assignment.   <u>   </u>

    c. The student turned in his composition.   <u>   </u>

2. Read the composition. **True** or **False**? Write a question mark (**?**) if the information isn't in the composition.

>   I arrived in this country in 1997. I c~~o~~me *a* with my parents, my brother, and my little sister. At first I wasn't very happy. I didn't know anyone beside~s~ my family, and I missed my friends a lot. My mother told me, "Don't worry! Things will get better."
>
>   When I began ~~the~~ school, things improved a little. I made some friends right away. We studied together and spent time together on the weekends. Since we were all from different countries we had to speak English. That really helped a lot! Now I can even write a composition in English. I guess my mother was ~~write~~. *right*

    a. Someone edited the paper.   <u> True </u>

    b. This is a first draft.   <u>   </u>

    c. There are two paragraphs in this composition.   <u>   </u>

    d. There are only six sentences in the second paragraph.   <u>   </u>

    e. The student used question marks.   <u>   </u>

    f. The student used three apostrophes in the first paragraph.   <u>   </u>

    g. The student used a semicolon.   <u>   </u>

    h. There is a colon before the quotation marks.   <u>   </u>

    i. The period comes *before* the last quotation marks.   <u>   </u>

    j. The last sentence of the second paragraph ends with an exclamation mark.   <u>   </u>

    k. There are two commas in the second sentence of the first paragraph.   <u>   </u>

    l. The student turned in his paper late.   <u>   </u>

3. What about you? Check (✔) the things you usually do when you write a composition.

    ☐ write a first draft   ☐ edit it   ☐ get feedback   ☐ rewrite the paper before I turn it in

Challenge   Write a composition of three paragraphs about how you felt when you came to this country or started this school. Write a first draft, edit it, get feedback, rewrite it, and turn it in to your teacher.

1. Look in your dictionary. Complete the chart. There is more than one right answer for each!

		EXAMPLE	YEAR(S)
a.	Exploration	Armstrong on the moon	1969
b.	War		
c.	Immigration		
d.	Movement		
e.	Election		
f.	Invention		

2. Circle the letter of the correct answer. Use your dictionary for help.

History 101

Name _____

1. Edison invented the lightbulb in _____ .

    a. 1875   **(b.)** 1879   **c.** 1890

2. Kennedy was assassinated _____ the war in Vietnam.

    a. before   **b.** during   **c.** after

3. The first group of Hungarians came to the U.S. _____ the Japanese.

    a. before   **b.** after   **c.** at the same time as

4. Before 1700, the U.S. Native American population was _____ .

    a. less than a million   **b.** a million   **c.** more than a million

5. World War I lasted about the same number of years as _____ .

    a. the Civil War   **b.** the war in Vietnam   **c.** World War II

6. The Internet became popular in _____ .

    a. 1970   **b.** 1980   **c.** 1990

7. Slavery was abolished the same year as _____ .

    a. the Battle of Wounded Knee   **b.** Lincoln's assassination   **c.** the invention of the telephone

8. Middle Easterners began to immigrate to the U.S. at the same time as _____ .

    a. Southeast Asians   **b.** Central Americans   **c.** Russians

---

3. Complete the paragraphs with the name of the events in the box. Write the dates in parentheses ( ). Use your dictionary for help.

Bill of Rights	**Civil War**	**The Depression**	**Cherokee Trail of Tears**
	Louisiana Purchase	~~**United Nations**~~	

DID YOU KNOW...?

a. The founders of the _____United Nations_____
(____1945____) chose New York City as its home, but the land and buildings are in an international zone. It has its own flag, post office, stamps, and security. Today, more than 150 countries are members of this organization for peace.

b. When President Thomas Jefferson made the _____
(_____), he added almost a million square miles to the United States. The United States paid France about $15,000,000 for the land.

c. The state government of Georgia made Native Americans leave their homes and walk the long distance to Oklahoma. Thousands of people died on the _____ (_____) because of disease and cold weather.

d. The stock market crash in 1929 started _____ , which lasted ten years (_____). During that time, 25 percent of all workers couldn't find jobs.

e. The _____ between the North and South lasted four years (_____). Almost 500,000 people died—more than the total number of deaths in all other wars fought in the United States.

f. The first ten amendments, or changes, to the U.S. Constitution are called the _____ (_____). They guarantee freedom of religion, speech, and the press. They also promise a trial by jury to any person accused of a crime.

4. What about you? Draw a time line, like the one in your dictionary, for some of the major events in your country's history. Use your own paper.

Challenge Look in your dictionary. Choose two events. Look them up in an almanac, encyclopedia, or history textbook. Write paragraphs like the ones in Exercise 3.

U.S. Government and Citizenship

1. Look in your dictionary. Complete the information about the U.S. government.

There are three ___branches___ of
a.
government: the _____, the
b.
legislative, and the judicial.

Every four years, U.S. citizens vote for

_____, the most important
c.
person in the executive branch. He or she lives in

_____ and "manages" the
d.
country. If the president dies or becomes too sick

to work, the _____ continues to
e.
do the job.

The _____ branch, called
f.
Congress, makes the laws of the country. It has two

"houses": _____ and the
g.
House of Representatives. The Senate has 100

members called _____. There
h.
are two from each state and they are elected for

six-year terms. The House has 435 members called

_____ or _____.
i. **j.**

States with bigger populations have more

representatives than states with smaller populations.

These representatives are elected for two-year terms.

The third branch of government, the

_____ branch, reviews laws to
k.
make sure they agree with the U.S. Constitution. The

highest court is called _____. Its
l.
decisions are final. Eight _____
m.
and one _____ "sit" on the
n.
Supreme Court. When there is an empty seat, the

president chooses a judge. After the Senate approves

the choice, the judge can keep his or her job for life.

2. Circle the correct words to complete the sentences.

a. You must be (18)/ 21 years old to take a U.S. citizenship test.

b. You have to live in the U.S. for _five / fifteen_ years to become a citizen.

c. U.S. citizens can vote for _chief justice / president_.

d. U.S. citizens pay taxes _every year / every four years_.

e. Both men and women must _obey the law / register with the Selective Service_.

f. _Citizens / Judges_ serve on a jury.

Challenge Compare a branch of the U.S. government with another country's government that you know. **Example:** *In the United States, a president runs the country. In Jordan, a king does.*

1. Look in your dictionary. **True** or **False**? Correct the underlined words in the false sentences.

   a. There's a waterfall in the ~~forest~~.   *rain forest*   _____False_____

   b. An ocean is <u>larger</u> than a pond and a bay.   _____

   c. A <u>peninsula</u> has water all around it.   _____

   d. There's a <u>canyon</u> between the mountains.   _____

   e. There are flowers in the <u>valley</u>.   _____

   f. There is a <u>mountain range</u> in the desert.   _____

   g. Hills are <u>lower</u> than mountains.   _____

2. Complete the descriptions. Use the words in the box. Look at the world map on **pages 124 and 125** in your dictionary if you need help.

desert	island	lake	mountain peak	ocean	river	~~waterfall~~

   ## WORLD FACTS

   a. **Angel Falls** (3,212 feet) is the highest _____*waterfall*_____ in the world. It is located on the Churun River in southeast Venezuela.

   b. The **Pacific** is the largest (64,186,300 square miles) and the deepest (12,925 feet) _____ in the world. It covers almost one third of the earth's surface.

   c. Located in Tibet and Nepal, **Everest** (29,028 feet) is the highest _____ in the world. In 1953, Hillary and Norgay were the first to reach the top.

   d. At 4,160 miles, the **Nile**, in Africa, is the longest _____ in the world. Water from the Nile supplies electricity and helps agriculture in Egypt and the Sudan.

   e. The **Sahara** in Africa is the biggest _____ in the world. At 3,500,000 square miles, it is almost as large as the United States. It gets only from five to ten inches of rain a year and sometimes has dry periods that last for years.

   f. Surrounded by water, **Greenland** (840,000 square miles) is the largest _____ in the world. It lies in the Arctic Circle and is a part of Denmark, although it is 1,300 miles away.

   g. The **Caspian Sea** (144,000 square miles) is the largest _____ in the world. It's called a sea because its water is salty.

Challenge Write some facts about a rain forest, a canyon, and a peninsula.

Mathematics

1. Look in your dictionary. Complete the diagram.

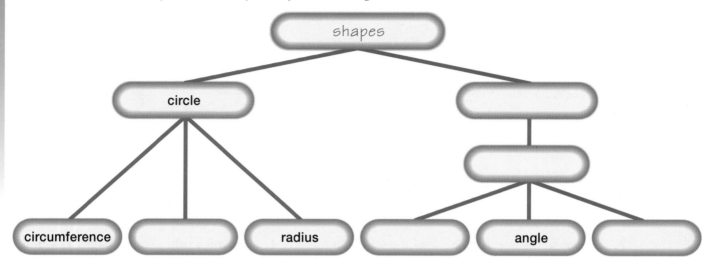

shapes

circle

circumference   radius   angle

2. Circle the correct words to complete the sentences.

a. A rectangle / square has four equal sides.

b. An oval / A triangle has three sides.

c. The diameter is always longer / shorter than the radius.

d. A diagonal line is curved / straight.

e. The distance between two parallel / straight lines is always equal.

f. Parallel / Perpendicular lines sometimes look like the letter T.

g. The type of mathematics that studies shapes is called geometry / trigonometry.

h. A cube / square is a solid.

3. Complete the analogies.

a. circle : sphere = square : _____ *cube* _____

b. triangle : three = rectangle : _____

c. addition : subtraction = multiplication : _____

d. oval : shape = cone : _____

e. triangle : shape = _____ : solid

f. division : quotient = subtraction : _____

4. What about you? Which operations or types of math do you use? When do you use them?

Example: *I use multiplication to change dollars to pesos.*

_____

_____

_____**Challenge** Draw a circle. Include the diameter and the radius. Write the measurements. Calculate the circumference. (Circumference = diameter × π)

118

1. Look in your dictionary. Write the type of science class on these notes.

a.

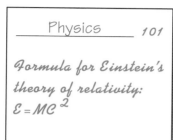

_____Physics_____ 101

Formula for Einstein's theory of relativity:

$E = MC^2$

b.

_____ 101

$H_2 + Cl_2 \rightarrow 2HCl$
(2 atoms of hydrogen + 2 atoms of chlorine → 2 molecules of hydrochloric acid)
<u>Lab assignment</u>: Do experiment on p. 23. Record the results.
<u>Must</u> wear goggles!

c.

_____ 101

Lab: Examine slide of frog's egg through microscope.
Bring dissection kit for tomorrow.

2. Complete the list of laboratory equipment. Use the words in the box.

| balance | Bunsen burner | ~~crucible tongs~~ | forceps | funnel | graduated cylinder |

a. ____crucible tongs____ : to pick up hot objects

b. _____ : to hold large amounts of material

c. _____ : to heat substances

d. _____ : to weigh chemicals

e. _____ : to pour liquids into a narrow container

f. _____ : to pick up very small things

3. Look at the lab experiment. Complete the list of laboratory equipment.

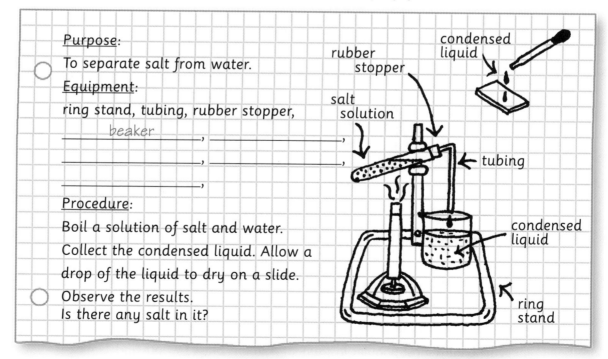

<u>Purpose</u>:
○ To separate salt from water.
<u>Equipment</u>:
ring stand, tubing, rubber stopper,
_____beaker_____, _____,
_____, _____,
_____,

<u>Procedure</u>:
Boil a solution of salt and water.
Collect the condensed liquid. Allow a drop of the liquid to dry on a slide.
○ Observe the results.
Is there any salt in it?

Challenge Look at **page 185** in this book. Follow the instructions.

Music

1. Look in your dictionary. Cross out the word that doesn't belong. Write the category.

a. _____brass_____   French horn   ~~bass~~   trombone   tuba

b. _____   clarinet   tambourine   piano   drums

c. _____   cello   violin   guitar   organ

d. _____   flute   oboe   xylophone   saxophone

2. Look at the bar graph. Circle the correct words to complete the sentences.

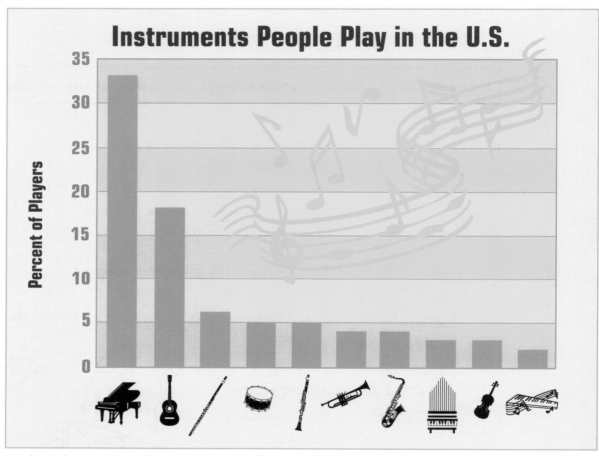

Based on information from: Heymann, T.: *The Unofficial U.S. Census.* (NY: Ballantine Books, 1991)

a. Almost 20 percent of players play the (guitar)/ violin .

b. The electric keyboard / piano is the most popular instrument.

c. More people play the flute / saxophone than the drums.

d. The trumpet is not as popular as the clarinet / saxophone .

e. Fewer than five percent of players play the flute / organ .

f. The saxophone is as popular as the clarinet / trumpet .

g. The third most popular instrument is in the brass / woodwind family.

Challenge   Ask your classmates about the instruments they play. Draw a bar graph like the one in Exercise 2.

1. Look in your dictionary. Write the school subject for each course description. Read quickly. You don't need to understand every word!

Courses

a. <u>Computer Science</u>   This basic class introduces students to hardware and software systems, and applications such as Microsoft® Word and Microsoft® Excel. There are two hours of lecture and two hours of lab each week.

b. _____ Three levels of ESL classes are offered in Conversation, Grammar, Reading, and Writing. In addition to three hours of class, there are two half-hour language lab sessions each week.

c. _____ Classes are offered in Spanish, French, and Japanese. Students learn grammar, conversation, reading, and writing. In addition to three hours of class, there are two half-hour language lab sessions each week.

d. _____ Students study plays and practice basic acting techniques, directing, and stage design. At the end of the school year they perform in a one-act play.

e. _____ Students choose among a variety of fitness and sports activities including basketball, volleyball, weightlifting, and aerobics. Activities take place in the gym and on the track. Two days a week. Proper sports clothing is required.

f. _____ This class, which meets after school hours, prepares students to pass the road test. After passing the written part of the test, students receive instruction behind the wheel. Must be 16 years old and have parents' permission.

g. _____ Students learn to operate common hand- and power-tools and to make basic home repairs, including car repairs.

h. _____ Basic drawing and painting. No experience necessary.

i. _____ Students learn basic concepts of money and credit, profit and loss, supply and demand, business cycles, banking, and the stock market.

j. _____ Students learn basic cooking skills (knife-cutting skills, measuring ingredients, cooking methods, menu planning) and sewing techniques.

k. _____ Students learn office procedures and skills such as dictation, keyboarding, and use of the fax, the adding machine, and other office equipment.

l. _____ Students learn how to read music and sing a variety of songs from rock to opera. They perform at holidays and graduation.

2. What about you? Look at the classes in Exercise 1. Which classes do you think students should have to take (core courses)? Which classes do you think should be electives? Make two lists. Use your own paper.

Challenge Look at your lists in Exercise 2. Give reasons for your opinions.

1. Look in your dictionary. Cross out the word that doesn't belong. Complete the chart.

a. States in Mexico	~~Louisiana~~	Durango	Sonora	Jalisco
b. ___States___ in the United States	Florida	Hawaii	Michigan	Baja California
c. Provinces in _____	Alberta	Alaska	Nova Scotia	Québec
d. _____ in Central America	Belize	Guatemala	Ontario	Panama
e. Regions of Mexico	Atlantic Provinces	Yucatan Peninsula	Chiapas Highlands	Gulf Coastal Plain
f. _____ of the United States	Midwest	Prairie Provinces	West Coast	Rocky Mountains
g. Bodies of Water	Gulf of Mexico	Southern Uplands	Atlantic Ocean	Caribbean Sea
h. _____	Costa Rica	Puerto Rico	Cuba	Bahamas

2. Look in your dictionary. Complete these sentences.

a. Texas is in the _____southwest_____ region of the United States.

b. Nicaragua lies between _____ and _____ in Central America.

c. _____ and the Dominican Republic share the same Caribbean island.

d. _____ is the smallest Canadian province.

e. _____, Mexico is northwest of Coahuila.

f. The west side of the U.S. state of _____ lies on the Gulf of Mexico.

g. _____ is southwest of the U.S. state of Nebraska.

h. The U.S. state of _____ is made of many islands.

i. Campeche lies in the _____ region of Mexico.

j. _____ is the largest island in the Caribbean Sea.

3. Look at the map. It shows where some products of Mexico come from. **True** or **False**? Correct the underlined words in the false sentences. Use your dictionary for help.

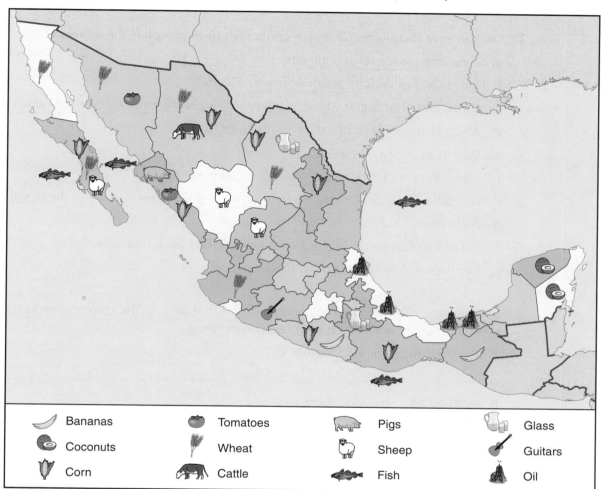

Bananas		Tomatoes		Pigs		Glass
Coconuts		Wheat		Sheep		Guitars
Corn		Cattle		Fish		Oil

                             north

a. Tomatoes are grown in the ~~south~~ of Mexico.   *False*

b. <u>Coconuts</u> grow in the Yucatan Peninsula.   _____

c. Bananas grow in the <u>north</u> of Mexico.   _____

d. Fishing is done in both the <u>Gulf of Mexico</u> and the <u>Pacific Ocean</u>.   _____

e. Oil is found in the <u>west</u>.   _____

f. There is <u>more</u> wheat in the north than in the south.   _____

g. Guitars are made in <u>Michoacan</u>.   _____

h. <u>Pigs</u> are raised in Sinaloa.   _____

4. What about you? Draw a map showing some of the products of your country. Write eight sentences. Use your own paper.

Challenge Look at the map in Exercise 3. Write five more sentences about Mexican products.

The World

1. Look in your dictionary. Circle the correct words to complete the sentences.

   a. There are six /(seven) continents.

   b. Tanzania is in Africa / South America .

   c. Greenland, the biggest island in the world, is part of Europe / North America .

   d. Africa is bigger / smaller than South America.

   e. Syria is in Africa / Asia .

   f. Chad, in central Africa, has five / six neighbors.

   g. Located on two continents, China / Russia is the biggest country in the world.

   h. Afghanistan, in Asia, has five / six neighbors.

   i. Poland, in Europe, is bigger / smaller than the Czech Republic.

   j. Kazakhstan / Turkey is on the Black Sea.

2. Look in your dictionary. Write comparisons with *than*. Use the correct form of the words in parentheses ( ). Choose your own comparison for **g**.

   a. IN AFRICA: Uganda / Angola (big)

   Angola is bigger than Uganda. _____

   b. IN EUROPE: Italy / Finland (warm)

   _____

   c. IN ASIA: Thailand / Laos (small)

   _____

   d. IN SOUTH AMERICA: Chile / Argentina (wide)

   _____

   e. AUSTRALIA / ANTARCTICA (cold)

   _____

   f. NEAR SOUTH ASIA: The Red Sea / The Arabian Sea (narrow)

   _____

   g. IN NORTH AMERICA: _____ / _____ (_____)

   _____

3. Look in your dictionary. For each continent, find a country that is landlocked (it has no water around it).

   Africa: _____ Chad _____   South America: _____

   Europe: _____   Asia: _____

4. Look in your dictionary. Complete these world facts. Write the names of the countries and the bodies of water.

a. _____ Mexico _____

Location: southern North America

Borders: U.S. to north, Gulf of Mexico to east, Belize and Guatemala to south, _____ Ocean to west

b. _____

Location: island off southeast Africa in western _____ Ocean

Borders: about 300 miles (500 km) east of Mozambique

c. _____

Location: central Europe

Borders: Germany and Czech Republic to north, Hungary and Slovakia to east, Slovenia and _____ to south, Switzerland and Liechtenstein to west

d. Laos

Location: southeast Asia

Borders: Myanmar to northwest, _____ to north, Vietnam to east, Cambodia to south, _____ to southwest

e. _____

Location: Western Africa

Borders: Guinea to north, Atlantic Ocean and _____ to west, Ivory Coast to east

f. _____

Location: northwestern South America

Borders: Colombia to north, Peru to east and south, _____ to west

g. Belarus

Location: northeastern Europe

Borders: Lithuania and _____ to north and northwest; Russia to north, northeast, and east; _____ to south, Poland to west

h. _____

Location: southwestern Asia

Borders: Turkmenistan to northwest, Tajikistan to north, China to northeast, Pakistan to east and south, _____ to west

5. What about you? Write a description of your country like the ones in Exercise 4. (If your country is in Exercise 4, choose a country you have visited.) Use your own paper.

Challenge Choose five other countries. Write descriptions like the ones in Exercise 4.

Energy and the Environment

1. Look in your dictionary. Circle the correct words to complete these sentences.

   a. Nuclear /(Solar) energy comes directly from the sun.

   b. Coal, oil, and natural gas / radiation are sources of energy.

   c. Another source of energy is acid rain / wind.

   d. Hydroelectric power / Geothermal energy comes from water.

   e. A danger of nuclear energy is radiation / smog.

   f. Old batteries / Paper bags are examples of hazardous waste.

   g. Acid rain / An oil spill kills trees.

   h. ✪ means radiation / recycle.

2. Look at suggestions for ways to save the earth. Check (✓) the correct column(s).

	HELP SAVE...			HELP PREVENT...			
	Energy	Water	Trees	Air Pollution	Water Pollution	Hazardous Waste	Pesticide Poisoning
a. Buy a "low-flow" showerhead.	✓	✓					
b. Use less detergent.					✓		
c. Use public transportation.							
d. Recycle newspapers.							
e. Keep refrigerator at 38°–40°F, not lower.							
f. Turn the faucet off while you brush your teeth.							
g. Get your car checked regularly.							
h. Recycle batteries or use rechargeable ones.							
i. Turn off lights when you're not using them.							
j. Use "natural" methods to control cockroaches, ants, etc.							

3. What about you? List the things in Exercise 2 that you do. Use your own paper.

   Example: *I use public transportation to save energy and help prevent air pollution.*

   Challenge List other things people can do to help save the earth.

1. Look in your dictionary. Complete the chart.

Planet Name	Symbol	Distance from the Sun (in miles)	Diameter (in miles)
a. _____Mars_____	♂	142 million	4,220
b. _____	♀	67 million	7,521
c. _____	⊕	93 million	7,926
d. _____	♄	888 million	74,975
e. _____	♇	3.6 billion	1,429
f. _____	♃	484 million	88,732
g. _____	☉	1.8 billion	31,763
h. _____	♆	2.8 billion	30,755
i. _____	☿	36 million	3,031

2. Circle the correct words to complete these sentences. You can use your dictionary for help.

a. There are nine moon / (planets) / stars in the solar system.

b. Uranus was the first planet discovered with a magnet / microscope / telescope .

c. The astronaut / astronomer / space station William Herschel first observed Uranus in 1781.

d. Thousands of asteroids / constellations / galaxies orbit the sun between Mars and Jupiter.

e. Constellations / Galaxies / Comets look like pictures in the sky.

f. The Earth's galaxy / orbit / space (a group of billions of stars) is called the Milky Way.

g. It takes 27 days for the moon to go from a new moon to a full moon and back to

a crescent moon / new moon / quarter moon again.

3. What about you? Describe what you can see when you look at the night sky. Use your own paper.

Example: *I can see the constellation called the Big Dipper...*

Challenge Look in an encyclopedia, almanac, or science book. Find out more about three planets. How long does a day last? How long does it take to orbit the sun?

▶ **Go to page 178 for Another Look (Unit 9).**

Trees and Plants

1. Look in your dictionary. Which trees or plants have…? You will use some answers more than once.

COLORFUL FLOWERS	BERRIES	NEEDLES	LEAVES THAT CAN GIVE YOU A RASH
dogwood	poison sumac	redwood	poison oak

2. Circle the correct words to complete the article. You can use your dictionary for help.

Trees

Trees are the biggest flowers / **plants** in the world. As long as they live, they never stop growing. The tallest tree, the pine / redwood, can reach a height of 368 feet. Its cone / trunk can have a diameter of 15 feet.
  a.   b.   c.

The limbs / roots, which grow underground, are the fastest growing part of a tree. They collect water and send it up the berries / trunk to the leaves / vines.
  d.   e.   f.

There are two main categories of trees. *Broad-leaf trees*, such as the maple / pine, have leaves that turn beautiful colors and then drop to the ground in the fall. They often have many large branches that grow from the lower trunk.
  g.

Needle-leaf trees, such as the birch / pine, stay green all year and are called evergreens. They carry seeds in cones / berries. The trunk / twig usually goes to the top of the tree.
  h.   i.   j.

A third category of tree is the *elm / palm*. It is almost all leaves / limbs and does not have branches / roots.
  k.   l.
  m.

All trees have flowers. Some are very colorful and beautiful like those of the magnolia / willow. Others, such as those of the dogwood / oak, are so small that many people do not notice them.
  n.   o.

Challenge Make a list of at least five tree products.

128

1. Look in your dictionary. Complete the order form for this bouquet.

Westside 🌹 *Florist*

Order Form

1 mixed bouquet:

a. 4   purple tulips
b.   pink
c. 3
d. 1
e.   yellow
f.

2. Look in your dictionary. Complete the sentences with information from the chart.

FLOWER	GROWN FROM	SEASON	COMMENTS
		spring–fall	remove thorns for bouquets
		late spring–late summer	water often
		summer–early winter	plant seedlings in June
		early spring	very short stems
		October–June	3–4 buds on each stem
		winter–spring	good houseplant
		spring–summer	lovely perfume

a. _____Lilies_____ and _____ grow from bulbs.

b. _____, _____, and _____ grow from seeds.

c. _____ have thick white petals and smell very nice.

d. You can buy _____ in the spring, fall, and all winter.

e. Don't hurt your finger when you make a bouquet of _____ !

Challenge   Write about flower traditions in your country. **Example:** *In the United States, men often give red roses to their wives or girlfriends on Valentine's Day.*

Marine Life, Amphibians, and Reptiles

1. Look in your dictionary. Match the animals that look similar. Write the numbers.

__3__	**a.** frog	**1.** garter snake
_____	**b.** salamander	**2.** porpoise
_____	**c.** dolphin	**3.** toad
_____	**d.** walrus	**4.** crocodile
_____	**e.** alligator	**5.** lizard
_____	**f.** eel	**6.** sea lion

2. Complete the conversations at an aquarium. Use the words in the box. Use your dictionary for help.

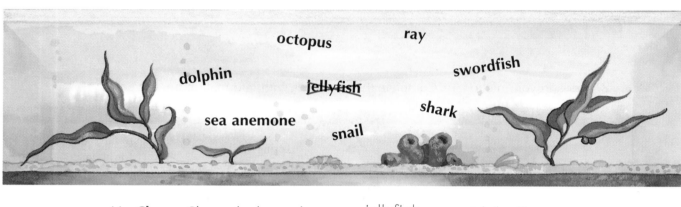

octopus   ray   dolphin   ~~jellyfish~~   swordfish   sea anemone   shark   snail

a. Ms. Chen: Class, who knows how _____jellyfish_____ catch food?

    Tina: Those long strings hanging down are poisonous. They kill small sea animals that swim through them.

b. Kim: Is that a flower?

    Ms. Chen: No, it's an animal. It's called a _____.

c. Steven: What's that flat, green fish with the long tail?

    Larry: I think it's a _____.

d. Dion: What a long nose! Is it sharp?

    Ms. Chen: Sure. That's why that fish is called a _____.

e. Ms. Chen: Look, Shannon. That animal doesn't have any gills. Is it a fish?

    Shannon: No, it's a _____. That's a kind of mammal.

f. Ms. Chen: How many legs does the _____ have?

    Abdul: Eight.

g. Tara: What's that large fish with the fin on the middle of its back?

    Ms. Chen: It's a _____.

h. Todd: Is that sea animal with the dark brown shell dead?

    Ms. Chen: No, it just moves very slowly. That's why people say "as slow as a _____."

3. Circle the correct words to complete the article.

Animal Defenses

Animals have many ways of protecting themselves. Some have colors that make them hard to

see. One fish, the cobra / (flounder), can change its color to match the environment. Two sea animals,
        a.

the squid / sea lion and the otter / octopus, squirt ink into the water and hide in its dark cloud.
        b.   **c.**

Some poisonous amphibians / gills and reptiles warn enemies to keep away. For example,
                d.

the bright colors of some frogs / fins tell other animals that they are not safe
                e.

to eat, and the garter snake / rattlesnake makes a loud sound with the end of
                f.

its tail before it bites. The turtle's / trout's hard shell and the sharp needles of
                g.

the sea urchin / anemone are another kind of protection.
        h.

Sea mammals like dolphins / swordfish are intelligent and use language to warn each other of
                i.

danger. Scientists have even recorded the songs that whales / worms sing to each other as they
                                        j.

travel around the world. Other members of this group, such as walruses and sea lions / sea horses,
                                                k.

live in large communities to protect their babies.

4. Circle the correct letter for each statement. Write the letters in the circles below. You can use your dictionary for help.

	TRUE	FALSE
a. Salamanders have fur.	A	(O)
b. Whales can swim.	L	Z
c. All sea mammals have gills.	J	O
d. Some mammals have fins.	R	L
e. Rattlesnakes are poisonous.	E	B
f. All reptiles have legs.	G	C
g. Bass have scales.	D	P
h. Scallops and shrimp are black.	E	I
i. Jellyfish look like fish.	T	C

(O) ◯ ◯ ◯ ◯ ◯ ◯ ◯ ◯

Now unscramble the letters to find the name of an animal: _____

Challenge Look at **page 185** in this book. Follow the instructions.

Birds, Insects, and Arachnids

1. Look in your dictionary. Complete the diagram with the words in the box.

~~feathers~~ claws six or eight legs a beak two legs wings

Both

Birds   **Insects and Arachnids**

feathers

2. Look in your dictionary. Write the name of the bird, insect, or arachnid.

a. It makes honey from flowers. Unlike the wasp, it dies after it stings.   _honeybee_

b. It looks like a big duck and is raised for food and feathers.   _____

c. It's very small. It eats blood and often lives in the fur or skin of mammals. It can make people sick.   _____

d. It's brown with an orange breast.   _____

e. It's very small and red, and it has black polka dots.   _____

f. It has sharp claws and big eyes in the front of its head.   _____

g. It begins its life as a caterpillar.   _____

h. It has a long bill for eating nectar from flowers. It moves its wings 1,000 times a second.   _____

i. It catches insects by making holes in trees with its beak.   _____

j. It doesn't fly, but swims in icy water to catch fish.   _____

k. It lives near water. It flies and bites people.   _____

l. It looks like a small grasshopper, and eats cloth like a moth. It makes music by rubbing its wings together.   _____

m. It has beautiful blue feathers and eats insects and fruit.   _____

n. It likes human food and causes many diseases. A spider often catches it in its web.   _____

o. It's very big with long, colorful feathers.   _____

3. What about you? What are some common birds, insects, and arachnids where you live? Make a list. Use your own paper.

Challenge Look up information about a bird, insect, or arachnid in your list from Exercise 3. Where does it live? What does it eat? How does it help or hurt people?

1. Look in your dictionary. Which animals…?

a. are babies ___kitten___ _____

b. have wings _____ _____ _____

c. live in water _____

d. have stripes _____

e. live in holes _____

f. give us milk _____ _____ _____

g. lay eggs _____

h. carry people _____ _____

2. Look at the chart and complete the sentences.

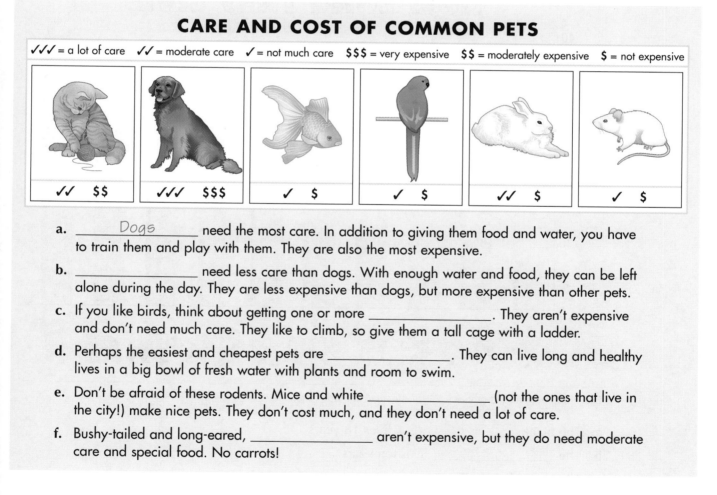

CARE AND COST OF COMMON PETS

✓✓✓ = a lot of care ✓✓ = moderate care ✓ = not much care $$$ = very expensive $$ = moderately expensive $ = not expensive

✓✓ $$ ✓✓✓ $$$ ✓ $ ✓ $ ✓✓ $ ✓ $

a. ___Dogs___ need the most care. In addition to giving them food and water, you have to train them and play with them. They are also the most expensive.

b. _____ need less care than dogs. With enough water and food, they can be left alone during the day. They are less expensive than dogs, but more expensive than other pets.

c. If you like birds, think about getting one or more _____. They aren't expensive and don't need much care. They like to climb, so give them a tall cage with a ladder.

d. Perhaps the easiest and cheapest pets are _____. They can live long and healthy lives in a big bowl of fresh water with plants and room to swim.

e. Don't be afraid of these rodents. Mice and white _____ (not the ones that live in the city!) make nice pets. They don't cost much, and they don't need a lot of care.

f. Bushy-tailed and long-eared, _____ aren't expensive, but they do need moderate care and special food. No carrots!

3. What about you? Have you ever had a pet? How did you care for it?

Example: *I have a dog. I walk it every morning before school…*

Challenge Look at **page 185** in this book and follow the instructions.

Mammals

1. Look in your dictionary. Which animals have these forms of protection?

   horns: _____buffalo_____ _____ _____

   quills: _____

   antlers: _____ _____

   tusks: _____

   a bad smell: _____

   Name two other
   forms of protection: _____ _____

2. Look at the bar graph. Complete the sentences.

Based on information from: *The World Almanac and Book of Facts 1998*. (NJ: World Almanac Books, 1997)

   a. The black _____bear_____ lives 18 years.

   b. The _____ lives ten years.

   c. The camel lives as long as the _____ .

   d. The black _____ lives five years longer than the giraffe.

   e. The _____ lives just as long as the rhinoceros and the _____ .

   f. The gorilla lives 13 years longer than the _____ .

   g. The _____ lives the longest.

3. Look at the pictures. Make a list of endangered* animals and the continent(s) where they live.

*there are very few, and they may not continue to live
Based on information from the Fish and Wildlife Service, U.S. Dept. of Interior, as of 1998

__bat, North America__

_____   _____

_____   _____

_____   _____

_____   _____

_____   _____

Challenge List reasons why some animals are endangered. You can use an encyclopedia for help. (Look up _endangered species._) **Example:** _People kill elephants for their tusks._

▶ **Go to page 179 for Another Look (Unit 10).**

1. Look in your dictionary. Write the job titles.

Help Wanted
a. _Dentist_
to examine, clean, and repair teeth, and treat diseases of the mouth at our East Side clinic. Saturdays and evening hours. 555-3443
b. _baker_
to make bread, pies, and cakes at our midtown restaurant. $6.67/ hr. 555-2343

Help Wanted
c. _doctor_
to examine and treat patients at busy medical clinic. 555-0432
d. _butcher_
to prepare and sell meat at our busy counter. S&W Supermarket.
$15,000/yr.
Call 555-4345

Help Wanted
e. _cashier_
to receive payment, give change and receipts to customers. Douglas Drugstore, Mineral Springs Road. 555-2243
f. _architect_
to plan and design public buildings at our growing firm.
McKAY, BROWN & PETRILLO
555-3451

2. Look at the bar graph. Circle the correct words to complete the sentences.

How Stressful* Is the Job?

*A *stressful* job is one that can make you feel nervous and not relaxed.
Based on information from: Krantz, L.: *Jobs Rated Almanac.* (NY: John Wiley & Sons, Inc., 1995)

According to the bar graph…

a. a doctor / (firefighter) has the job with the most stress.

b. a florist / computer programmer has the job with the least stress.

c. a doctor's job is (more) / less stressful than a dentist's job.

d. a hairdresser has a little less job stress than a garment worker / graphic artist has.

e. the garment worker, hairdresser, and computer programmer / dentist have about the same amount of stress.

3. Look in your dictionary. Write the job titles.

Help Wanted

g. _Caregiver_
to watch our two preschoolers. Good storytelling skills a must! Excellent references required. $10/hr. 555-3406

h. _cook_
to plan menus and prepare meals at our small Mexican restaurant. Work closely with servers and restaurant manager. La Paloma. 345 Riverside Avenue

i. _bricklayer_
to build walls, fireplaces, patios, etc. C&O Construction. 555-9723

j. _____
to put together parts in radio factory.
ON-THE-JOB-TRAINING
$250/wk.
call Frank Collins, 555-9922

Help Wanted

k. _____
to plan and supervise the building of roads, bridges, tunnels, and buildings.
FAX RESUME
555-3423

l. _____
to cut and arrange flowers.
THE ROSE BUD
Mon.–Sat. 10:00–6:00
555-4936

m. _____
to repair and maintain cars at small garage. Part-time, weekends.
555-7396

Help Wanted

n. _____
to help build shelves and doors in new building. $255/wk.
555-4345
Ask for Mr. Heller.

o. _____
to perform in plays for a small theater company. TV, stage, or movie experience.
555-8299

p. _____
to plan and organize appointments for busy business executive.
H. THOMAS & SONS
555-8787

Exciting opportunities exist at our new locations:

4. What about you? Compare these jobs. Which do you think is more interesting? more stressful?

a. cook / baker   _I think a baker's job is more interesting than a cook's job. A cook's job is probably more stressful._

b. engineer / carpenter   _____

c. assembler / dockworker   _____

d. caregiver / administrative assistant   _____

e. Other: _____ / _____   _____

Challenge Look at Exercise 4. Explain your choices.

1. Look in your dictionary. Cross out the word that doesn't belong. Give a reason.

   a.   receptionist   ~~model~~   secretary

   A model doesn't work in an office.

   b.   nurse   veterinarian   truck driver

   _____

   c.   mover   salesperson   stock clerk

   _____

   d.   welder   serviceman   machine operator

   _____

   e.   student   teacher   housekeeper

   _____

2. Read the conversations. Who's talking? Use the words in the box.

interpreter	~~instructor~~	lawyer	messenger	musician
police officer	receptionist	repair person	reporter	student
	telemarketer	travel agent		

   a. ___Instructor___ : There will be a math test on Monday.

   _____ : Can we use our calculators?

   b. _____ : Your honor, I object! My client is not guilty!

   _____ : Monsieur le juge, je récuse! Mon client n'est pas coupable!

   c. _____ : I'm Monica Stone, from Channel 5 news. Have you made any arrests,

   Detective Wong?

   _____ : We're questioning a suspect now.

   d. _____ : Hello. This is Dan from T & J Tools. We're selling excellent quality

   hammers at a great price.

   _____ : Thanks. But I don't use hammers when I work on TVs.

   e. _____ : I have to go to Miami tomorrow. I'm giving a concert.

   _____ : OK. Do you want a round-trip or one-way ticket?

   f. _____ : I've got a package for Bob Johnson.

   _____ : Mr. Johnson's office is the first door on your right.

3. Look at the chart. **True** or **False**?

Occupation	Hrs/Wk	$/Yr
	40	15,000
	45	50,000
	40	37,000
	40	21,000
	47.5	34,000
	47.5	26,000
	35	17,000
	50	69,000
	45	24,000
	45	25,000

Based on information from: Krantz, L.: *Jobs Rated Almanac.* (NY: John Wiley & Sons, Inc., 1995)

a. A repair person works longer hours than a nurse.   _True_

b. A server works as many hours as a painter.   _____

c. A painter works as many hours as a janitor.   _____

d. A veterinarian works the most hours and makes the most money.   _____

e. A server works the fewest hours and makes the least money.   _____

f. A musician makes two times as much as a writer.   _____

g. A police officer works longer than a nurse and makes more money.   _____

h. A welder works as many hours as a writer and makes almost as much money.   _____

4. What about you? Look at the chart in Exercise 3. Which jobs would or wouldn't you like? Why?

_____

_____

_____

_____

Challenge Look at **page 186** in this book. Complete the chart.

Job Skills

1. Look in your dictionary. Complete these job descriptions.

a. A cashier <u>uses a cash register</u> .

b. A chef _____ .

c. An orderly _____ .

d. A garment worker _____ .

e. A secretary _____ .

f. A server _____ .

g. An interpreter _____ .

h. A baby-sitter _____ .

2. What about you? Complete the questionnaire. Write your name and check (✓) the job skills you have.

CAN YOU...?	KIM	ALEXIS	CARLOS	DIANA	(Your Name)
use a cash register	✓				
work on a computer	✓			✓	
supervise people		✓			
speak another language	✓		✓	✓	
sell clothes		✓		✓	
repair appliances				✓	
operate heavy machinery			✓		
drive a truck		✓			
cook	✓				
do manual labor	✓		✓		
assemble parts		✓	✓		

3. Look at the chart in Exercise 2. **True** or **False**?

a. Kim could apply for a job as a chef. _____True_____

b. Carlos could get a job as a truck driver. _____

c. Diana could apply for a job as a secretary. _____

d. Only Diana could apply for a job as a repair person. _____

e. Both Kim and Alexis could get jobs as assemblers. _____

f. Alexis could apply for a job as a salesperson, but not as a repair person. _____

g. You could work as a cashier. _____

h. Both Diana and you could be managers. _____

i. You and Carlos can both work with your hands. _____

Challenge List three other job skills. Check (✓) the ones you and a classmate have.

Your Name _____   Classmate's Name _____

_____ ☐   ☐

_____ ☐   ☐

_____ ☐   ☐

1. Look in your dictionary. **Before** or **After**? Circle the correct word.

   a. Dan called for information (before)/ after he went on the interview.

   b. Before / After he talked to friends, he looked in the classifieds.

   c. Before / After he went on the interview, he filled out an application.

   d. Dan inquired about the salary before / after he talked about his experience.

2. Complete the information with the words in the box.

ask about benefits	ask about the hours	call for information	fill out an application
~~talk to friends~~	go on the interview	inquire about the salary	look at job boards
look in the classifieds	look for help wanted signs	talk about your experience	get hired

Looking for a Job

It can take a lot of time—and work—to find a job. Here are some tips.

Tell everyone that you are looking for work. Begin close to home. <u>Talk to friends</u>, relatives, teachers, and
                                                                    a.
classmates. Keep your eyes open. When you're walking down the street, _____ in store
                                                                                          b.
windows. _____ in school or in the supermarket. Get the newspaper every day and
             c.
_____ . But remember — "Help Wanted" ads do not tell you the whole story. You will probably
    d.
have to pick up the phone and _____ .
                                        e.
_____ : *Is the job 9:00 to 5:00? Do you have to work on weekends?*
    f.

Applying for a job When you apply for a job, you will probably have to _____ . This gives the
                                                                                    g.
employer basic information about your skills and experience. Then, when you _____ , you will
                                                                                    h.
have the chance to _____ in greater detail. The interviewer will ask you a lot of questions,
                            i.
but it's also important for **you** to ask questions.

_____ : *What's the starting pay?*
    j.

_____ : *What about health insurance?* Remember: Be patient and don't give up. You may
    k.
have to try many different approaches before you finally _____ and get that first paycheck!
                                                                    l.

3. What about you? Think about a time you or someone you know went on a job search. Write the steps. **Example:** *First, I looked at the classifieds. Then I…*

Challenge Look at **page 186** in this book. Follow the instructions.

An Office

1. Look in your dictionary. Cross out the word that doesn't belong. Give a reason.

a. office manager   ~~microcassette transcriber~~   secretary   file clerk

  A microcassette transcriber isn't a person.

b. desk   swivel chair   supply cabinet   pencil sharpener

  _____

c. rubber stamp   envelope   Post-it notes   notepad

  _____

d. paper clip   glue   rubber cement   paper cutter

  _____

e. fax machine   calculator   typewriter   stapler

  _____

2. Match the word parts. Write the numbers.

__5__	**a.** paper	**1.** pins
_____	**b.** correction	**2.** book
_____	**c.** postal	**3.** scale
_____	**d.** push	**4.** pad
_____	**e.** appointment	**5.** shredder
_____	**f.** legal	**6.** fluid

3. Read the notes. What do you need to do the job? Use the words from Exercise 2.

a.
> Hang this notice on the cafeteria bulletin board.
> Thanks.
> ♃

  pushpins

c.
> *This is for your eyes only! Please read and destroy.

  _____

e.
> I'll be out of the office on Friday. Please take notes at the staff meeting.
> —Thanks.
> R.F.

  _____

b.
> There are some mistakes in this report. Please correct them before you make copies.

  _____

d.
> Please let me know when my next meeting with L. J. Inc. is.

  _____

f.
> Mail two copies to Anne Miles.

  _____

4. Look at the picture and the instructions. What mistakes did the secretary make?

John—Type this report on letterhead paper. Make 3 copies, then collate and staple them. Leave them on my desk. Thanks.

R. Smith

Annual International Sales Conference

We are pleased to announce the plans for our Annual International Sales Conference. This year the conference will be held on April 20-23, in Miami, Florida, USA.

Catherine Hartman is in charge of the conference logistics. Her fax number is (212) 555-2121 and her telephone number is (212) 555-2100, ext. 321.

Catherine has prepared the attached information packet in which she has provided information about the costs of the conference as well as the weather in Miami in April and recommendations for clothing. She will send additional information about activities in which you

1

may wish to participate if you plan to be in Miami the weekend before the conference.

The conference headquarters will be at the Greatwood Hotel. We have had very good reports about this hotel from previous clients and visitors. Please fax the attached accommodations request form directly to the hotel by January 31. If you need to call the hotel, please ask for John Norton, the manager with whom we have made our arrangements.

Please book your own flights. Once you know the details, please fax the information to Catherine so she can arrange to have someone meet you at the airport.

If you have any questions about travel or accommodations, please call Catherine

2

M. SHAKTER

a. He didn't use letterhead. He used plain paper.

b. _____

c. _____

d. _____

e. _____

5. Circle the correct words to complete the instructions.

MEMO

To: Alice Rader   **From:** Marta Lopez

—The (photocopier) / mailer is broken again. Please call the repair person. You'll find the phone number
     a.
in the rotary card file / stacking tray under "r."
         b.

—Put the clients' names on the staples / labels before you file the papers on my desk.
                              c.

—Check my desk calendar / pad to see when the staff meetings are next month.
                 d.

—The book on my desk goes to A. Olinski at 354 Main Street. Use packing / clear tape so you can read
                                                            e.
the address through it.

—Before you file the Thompson report, use the paper cutter / shredder to make it 8 X 10 inches.
                                                 f.
It's too long now.

—Staple / Transcribe my notes from Tuesday's meeting. The microcassette / fax machine is on my desk.
   g.   **h.**

—Please stamp all letters to Japan "air mail." (The legal / ink pad is in the top left drawer.)
                                                   i.

Challenge Look at the office supplies in your dictionary. Which items can you use for the same job?
Example: *You can use a desk calendar or an appointment book to write appointments.*

Computers

1. Look in your dictionary. Complete the definitions from a user's manual.

INPUT (entering information)

   a. _____program_____ : (application) A type of software that tells the computer how to do different things (for example, doing math, playing games, making pictures).

   b. _____ : This looks like the part of a typewriter that has letters and numbers. You type on it to enter information into the computer.

PROCESSING (inside the computer)

   c. _____ : (central processing unit) This is the computer's "brain."

STORAGE (keeping information to use later)

   d. _____ : A small, square piece of plastic for saving information.

   e. _____ : A narrow opening in the computer for floppy disks.

   f. _____ : Inside the computer, it contains a disk that holds a lot of information.

OUTPUT (seeing your work)

   g. _____ : This looks like a TV screen. On it, you can read the words and numbers you type or see the charts and pictures you make.

   h. _____ : This gives you a "hard" or paper copy of your work.

COMMUNICATIONS (talking to other computers)

   i. _____ : This sends information from one computer to another over telephone lines.

   j. _____ : This special round disc holds a lot of information including pictures and sound. You can buy encyclopedias, dictionaries, and games in this form.

OTHER TERMS

   k. _____ : A small computer that uses batteries. Instead of a _____ , it has a trackball.

   l. _____ : This can "read" words and pictures from a book, newspaper, etc., into the computer without using a mouse or keyboard.

Challenge Write definitions for *power switch*, *cable*, and *port*.

144

1. Look in your dictionary. Complete these job descriptions. Write the job.

   a. Open and close the front lobby _____*door*_____ : _____*doorman*_____

   b. Supervise the bellhops: _____

   c. Register and check out _____ : _____

   d. Carry the guests' luggage on a luggage _____ : _____

   e. Clean rooms, _____ beds, and provide fresh towels: _____

2. Circle the correct words to complete this hotel brochure.

The Greatwood Hotel
Where great things happen!

Be our doorman /(guest!) For business or pleasure—everything you need...
    a.

Accommodations: We have 285 comfortable halls / guest rooms (non-smoking
    b.

available). Cable TV and VCR.

Food: Eat at our two restaurants and express breakfast buffet. Don't want to leave

your room? Call our 24-hour pool / room service.
    c.

Recreation: Swim in our heated outdoor lobby / pool. Work out in our health club.
    d.

Services and Features: Driving here? Enjoy our free housekeeping cart / valet parking.
    e.

Shop at our beautiful gift shop / luggage cart. Do business in our large
    f.

ballroom / meeting room. Dance to live music in our ballroom / meeting room.
    g.   **h.**

For more information or for reservations, call 800-555-9868

3. What about you? How important to you are these hotel features? Rank them.
(Number 1 = most important)

   _____ ice machine   _____ valet parking   _____ gift shop   _____ pool

   _____ ballroom   _____ room service   _____ meeting room   _____ doorman

Challenge Imagine you are staying at the hotel in your dictionary. Write a postcard to a friend.
Describe the hotel.

A Factory

1. Look in your dictionary. Complete the factory newsletter.

Vol. 25, No. 2
June 7, 2002

 **THE LAMPLIGHTER**

*Sun Electric
"We light up
your life"*

From the ___front office___
a.

T.J. Rolf, *President and* _____
b.

As we enter our 25th year of business, I want to thank

the following people for their dedication and hard work:

Ivonne Campis, _____
c.

For 15 years, Ivonne has assembled the

_____ that make our lamps. Her
d.

skill and care have contributed to the high quality of

our product.

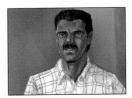

Prem Singh, _____
e.

For 10 years, Prem has watched over the assembly line,

assuring the highest product quality. He helps create a

friendly and productive work environment.

Alice Carver, _____
f.

Alice has worked in the _____ for
g.

5 years, taking finished lamps off the conveyor belt and

putting them in boxes ready for shipment.

**Employee of
the Month!**

Pete Tresante, *shipping clerk*

Pete has punched a time clock for more than 20 years.

He has stood on the _____ carefully
h.

checking the orders that we _____
i.

to over 32 states. Congratulations Pete!

Jan Larson, _____
j.

Jan has been hired to _____ a new
k.

desk lamp. We will begin to _____
l.

this new product in September. Welcome Jan!

Challenge Look in your dictionary. Write short paragraphs about the order puller and the forklift
operator for the factory newsletter in Exercise 1. Use your imagination.

1. Look in your dictionary. Write the name of the safety symbol for each hazard.

    a. a bottle of pesticide   _poison_

    b. a can of gasoline

    c. a used syringe

    d. an old car battery

    e. a nuclear medicine company

2. Circle the correct words to complete the safety poster.

WARNING

Protect Yourself from Head to Toe! Use Safety (Equipment) / Symbols!
a.

Protect your head: A hair net / hard hat
b.
can protect you from falling objects.

Don't forget your hair. If it's long, wear

a hair net / safety visor so it won't get
c.
caught in machinery.

Protect your eyes: Always wear safety

glasses / gloves or earmuffs / goggles
d.   e.
to protect your eyes from flying objects.

Protect your ears: Noise can cause hearing

loss. Wear earplugs / toe guards or safety
f.
earmuffs / goggles if you work near loud machinery.
g.

Protect your hands: Always wear work

or latex gloves / vests when handling
h.
hazardous / radioactive materials.
i.

Protect your feet: Always wear safety

work shoes or back supports / boots.
j.

Avoid dangerous situations: Don't use

power tools in wet locations or near

corrosive / flammable liquids or gases.
k.
Keep a fire extinguisher / toe guard
l.
on the wall.

Remember: Be careful / careless! Better safe than sorry!
m.

3. What about you? What safety equipment do you use? When do you use it?

    Example: _I wear earplugs when I go to a loud concert._

Challenge Look at **page 186** in this book. Follow the instructions.

Farming and Ranching

1. Look in your dictionary. Write an example of....

a. a type of livestock   _goats_

b. a crop used for feed   _____

c. a crop used to make clothing   _____

d. something that grows in a vegetable garden _____

e. something that grows in an orchard   _____

f. something that grows in a vineyard   _____

2. Circle the correct words to complete the letter.

Elmwood, Wisconsin

Dear Carlos,

My first day on the **farm** / ranch! When I got up, it was still dark. John
a.

Johnson, the <u>farmer / hired hand</u> who owns the place, was already in the
b.

<u>corral / barn</u>. He was <u>harvesting / milking</u> the cows. My job was to <u>feed / plant</u>
c. **d.** **e.**

the chickens and other <u>cattle / livestock</u>. I was happy when it was time for
f.

breakfast. We had fresh eggs and ham along with tomatoes from the

<u>vegetable garden / vineyard</u> and <u>rice / fruit</u> from the orchard.
g. **h.**

After breakfast, it was time to work in the <u>fence / field</u>. John says
i.

that in the old days horses pulled most of the <u>farm equipment / steers</u>. Today,
j.

a <u>hired hand / tractor</u> does the job. John and his <u>farmworkers / ranchers</u>
k. **l.**

planted rows of corn and other <u>crops / wheat</u>.
m.

It looks beautiful. They also grow <u>alfalfa / cotton</u>
n.

for animal feed. I'd like to come back when

they <u>harvest / milk</u> the corn in the summer.
o.

Life on the farm is hard work, but it's

great being outside, close to nature.

See you soon,

Jeff

    Challenge Would you like to spend some time on a farm or a ranch? Write a paragraph explaining
your opinion.

1. Look at the construction site in your dictionary. **True** or **False**? Correct the underlined words in the false sentences.

    a. There are ~~eight~~ *eleven* construction workers on the site.   _____False_____

    b. One worker is climbing a <u>ladder</u>.   _____

    c. Two construction workers are lifting <u>plywood</u>.   _____

    d. The <u>backhoe</u> is orange.   _____

    e. A worker is using a <u>sledgehammer</u> near the crosswalk.   _____

2. Complete the sentences. Use the words in the boxes.

insulation   bulldozer   crane   pickax   shovel   trowel   concrete

    a. You can use a _____*shovel*_____ to dig a small hole in the ground.

    b. A _____ moves earth or large rocks from one place to another.

    c. _____ keeps a house warm.

    d. A _____ can lift and place beams on high floors.

    e. A _____ and a _____ mixture are used to lay bricks.

    f. A _____ is used to dig in very hard ground.

3. What about you? Check (✓) the materials that your school and home are made of.

	SCHOOL BUILDING	HOME
bricks		
shingles		
stucco		
wood		
Other: _____		

Challenge Look for pictures of buildings in a newspaper, magazine, or in your picture dictionary. What building materials are used? **Example:** *The house on page 39 is made of brick.*

Tools and Building Supplies

1. Look in your dictionary. Cross out the word that doesn't belong. Then write the section of the hardware store.

   a. ___hardware___   nail   bolt   ~~outlet~~   screw
   b. _____   ax   plunger   pipe   fittings
   c. _____   circular saw   hammer   router   electric drill
   d. _____   brush   roller   spray gun   chisel
   e. _____   wire stripper drill bit   wire   extension cord
   f. _____   hacksaw   flashlight   wrench   mallet

2. Complete the conversations with the correct words from the box.

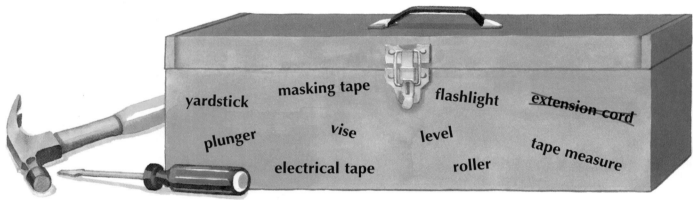

yardstick   masking tape   flashlight   ~~extension cord~~
plunger   vise   level   tape measure
electrical tape   roller

   a. **Ty:**   I want to plug in this electric drill, but it doesn't reach the outlet.
      Jade: No problem. Use this __extension cord__.

   b. **Ian:** I've been painting for hours and I still have three more walls to do.
      Tina: Why don't you use this _____? It's faster than a paintbrush.

   c. **Lily:** Oh, no. The toilet is stopped up again.
      Dan: Here. Use this _____. It always works.

   d. **Kim:** Do you know how long the shelf in the dining room is?
      Lian: No. Use the _____ or _____ to find out.

   e. **Eva:** Help! I could use a third hand here!
      Jana: Use the _____ to hold the wood in place.

   f. **Jules:** Don't get paint on the glass.
      Lyle: I won't. I put _____ around the panes before I started.

   g. **Nico:** That wire doesn't look very safe.
      Iris: Don't worry. I'll put some of this _____ on before using it.

   h. **Olga:** Does this shelf look straight?
      Boris: Hmm. I'm not sure. Let's use the _____. Then we'll know for certain.

   i. **Enzo:** It's so dark behind here. I can't see what I'm doing!
      Pia: Give me the _____. I'll hold it for you.

3. Look at the pictures. Each situation shows a mistake. Describe the mistake and tell the people what they need to do the job right.

a. *That's a Phillips screwdriver.*
You need the other kind.

b. _____
_____

c. _____
_____

d. _____
_____

e. _____
_____

4. What about you? Check (✓) the tools you have used (or someone you know has used). What did you use them for?

☐ hammer _____

☐ ax _____

☐ handsaw _____

☐ screwdriver _____

☐ pliers _____

☐ wrench _____

☐ vise _____

☐ electric drill _____

☐ Other: _____ _____

Challenge Imagine you can have only three tools from the ones in Exercise 4. Which would you choose? Explain your choice.

▶ **Go to page 180 for Another Look (Unit 11).**

Places to Go

1. Look in your dictionary. Complete the schedule.

What's Happening

Sports

Reds v. Kings baseball game ____ . 2:00, Sun.
                   a.

Hunter Field _____ , $8.
                b.

Art

Clark _____ . Special exhibit of
         c.

modern painting and _____ by
                      d.

American Artists. Fri. & Sat. 10–5, Sun. 1–5.

Children

Carousel Village. Home of the 120-ft. high

_____ . _____ by the
   e.   **f.**

Candycane Theater at 12, 1, & 2. Free with

admission to the _____ park.
                    g.

At _____
       h.

Independence Day*** (PG-13) Cinema 1,

Jack** (PG-13) Cinema 2.

Call 555-9347 for reserved

_____ , $7.
   i.

General Interest

• Vilas Park _____ . Elephants,
                j.

giraffes, and many other _____ .
                            k.

3:00 talk by _____ Sue Ray.
               l.

Daily 10–4. $5 adults, $2.50 children

(under age 3, free).

• Warwick _____ . More than 20
             m.

_____ selling clothes,
   n.

sunglasses, and other _____ .
                         o.

10–4 Sat. Free.

• Bayside _____ . More than 20
             p.

varieties of roses, and many other flowers.

Greenhouse tours daily, 11–4. Free.

• 23rd Street _____ . Games and
                 q.

rides. Weekends 11–4. Free.

• Tiverton _____ . Livestock
              r.

exhibitions, prizes. Free.

2. Look at the schedule in Exercise 1. Recommend events for these people.

a. Jack wants to be an announcer. ____baseball game____

b. David wants to be a gardener. _____

c. Julia needs some things for the house. _____

d. Ten-year-old Tina likes rides. _____ or _____

3. What about you? Look at the schedule in Exercise 1. Where would you like to go? Why?

Example: *I'd like to go to the zoo because I like animals.*

_____

_____

Challenge Look in a local newspaper. List four possible places to go next weekend. Rank them in
order of interest. (Number 1 = the most interesting) Explain your choices.

1. Look in your dictionary. Where can you hear…?

    a. "OK. Now, try to catch this."   _ball field_

    b. "Would you like some more chicken?"   _____

    c. "Look! They're swimming toward the bread!"   _____

    d. "Push me higher, Mommy!"   _____

    e. "Let's ride around one more time."   _____

    f. "Is that your pail and shovel?"   _____

    g. "Bring your arm all the way back when you serve the ball."   _____

2. Read about the children. What should they use? Use your dictionary for help.

    a. Toby likes to jump.   _jump rope_

    b. Jennifer is a little too young to ride a bicycle.   _____

    c. Timmy is thirsty.   _____

    d. Cindi likes to climb on bars.   _____

    e. Shao-fen likes to play on things that go up and down.   _____

    f. Carlos is tired and just wants to sit down and rest.   _____

3. What about you? Look at the park in your dictionary. What would you do there…?

    a. alone

        Example: _I would sit on a bench and watch the children._

        _____

    b. with a friend

        _____

    c. with three of your classmates

        _____

    d. with a three-year-old child

        _____

    e. with a ten-year-old child

        _____

    f. with a 65-year-old relative

        _____

Challenge Design the ideal park. What would it have? Write a description.

Outdoor Recreation

1. Look at the top picture in your dictionary. Find and correct six more mistakes in the letter. Do not change any of the number words.

Dear Robyn,

    Here's a picture of our first camping trip. (Tony just took it). As you can see, I'm cooking outside our tent. (That's me in front of the ~~camping stove~~ campfire.)

    Aren't the lake and mountains beautiful? Do you see the man fishing? He just caught something with his rope and fishing net. On the lake, two people are rafting, one person is boating in a small red motorboat, and three people are canoeing. Back on land, you can see people horseback riding and mountain biking. There are also three people hiking. One of them is sitting on a rock and resting. His life vest sure looks heavy! I'd prefer backpacking like those two people standing on the rocks in front of him.

    I'd better go. See you next week.   Becca

2. Read the conversations. What are they talking about? Use your dictionary for help.

a. **Ming:** *Brrr.* It's getting cold out here.

   Sue: Hand me <u>those</u>, and I'll light the fire.   <u>   matches   </u>

b. **Dave:** *Ow.* These mosquitoes are driving me crazy.

   Eva: Put some of <u>this</u> on.   <u>   </u>

c. **Bob:** I'm thirsty.

   Julie: I don't think there's any more water in <u>this</u>.   <u>   </u>

d. **Mia:** This rope is too long.

   Tom: Here. You can use <u>this</u> to cut it.   <u>   </u>

e. **Doug:** I can't sleep. The ground is really hard.

   Sarah: Why don't you put <u>this</u> under your sleeping bag?   <u>   </u>

f. **Luke:** It's really dark out here.

   Mike: Take <u>this</u> with you so you can see where you're going. <u>   </u>

3. What about you? Would you like to go camping? Why or why not?

Example: *I'd like to go camping. I like sleeping outside.*

_____

Challenge Look in your dictionary. Imagine you are on a camping trip. List the five most important items to have. Give reasons.

1. Look in your dictionary. Complete the sentences.

   a. The man and woman are wearing _____wet suits_____ and scuba tanks.

   b. The boy standing in the shade is wearing a diving mask and _____.

   c. There's a red _____ hanging from the lifeguard station.

   d. A woman is putting _____ on a little girl.

   e. The little girl in the pink bathing suit is listening to a _____.

2. Circle the correct words to complete this hotel ad.

The (Sand Castle)/Seashell Inn
a.

YOUR NUMBER ONE CHOICE FOR FUN IN THE SUN!

Relax under a beach <u>towel/umbrella</u> on our 1-mile white-sand <u>beach/pier</u>.
                b.   **c.**

Swim among the gentle <u>fins/waves</u> of our beautiful blue-green
                       d.

<u>ocean/scuba tank</u>. Eat inside our fine restaurant or buy a fresh fish
  e.

sandwich to put in your <u>bucket/cooler</u>.
                      f.

<u>Sailboats/Surfboards</u> and <u>scuba/rock</u> equipment available.
 g.   **h.**

For more information or for reservations call
1-800-555-SAND
or visit our WEB site at *www.sand_castle.com*

3. What about you? What would you take to the beach? What would you buy or rent at the beach? Check (✔) the columns.

	TAKE	BUY/RENT
surfboard		
beach umbrella		
beach chair		
beach towels		
sunblock		

	TAKE	BUY/RENT
cooler		
scuba tank		
fins		
pail		
Other: _____		

Challenge Imagine you are at the beach in your dictionary. Write a postcard describing it.
           Begin: *I'm sitting…*

Sports Verbs

1. Look in your dictionary at page 156. Write the sports verbs that complete the phrase: _____ *a ball.*

<u>   throw   </u>   <u>   </u>   <u>   </u>

<u>   </u>   <u>   </u>   <u>   </u>

<u>   </u>   <u>   </u>

2. Circle the correct words to complete the article.

SKI *or* SWIM? Getting and Staying Fit for Life

There are many choices for people who want to get and stay fit. Some sports require

very little special equipment. All you really need is a good pair of shoes to ski /(walk) your
a.

way to good health. And remember: Some experts say that it is better to walk fast than

to jog / kick or run. Walking, a "low-impact" sport, causes less stress to your bones and
b.

muscles. A water sport such as skiing / swimming is another good low-impact choice.
c.

But don't dive / dribble into a pool or lake unless you know the water is deep enough.
d.

And *never* go into the water alone.

Want to exercise / serve with other people? Many neighborhoods have gyms that
e.

you can join. There you can tackle / work out alone or with others. Bending and
f.

serving / stretching helps firm muscles and keep your body flexible.
g.

For those people who enjoy competing, there are many opportunities to race / pass in
h.

city marathons. But remember: Winning isn't everything. Even if you don't finish / start
i.

the race, feel good that you participated.

It's not really important which sport you choose. You can throw / shoot a baseball
j.

or ride / swing a bicycle. Just start slowly and be careful. (If you skate / ski, wear
k.   **l.**

a helmet and knee, wrist, and elbow pads.) Most of all, enjoy what you do and do it

regularly. In order to get and stay fit, sports should be a part of your everyday life.

3. Look in your dictionary. **True** or **False**? Correct the <u>underlined</u> words in the false sentences.

a. Two women in sweat suits are ~~running~~ *walking* in the park. _____False_____

b. Some teenage boys are <u>throwing and catching</u> a baseball. _____

c. Some <u>girls</u> are shooting baskets. _____

d. A woman is <u>bouncing</u> a tennis ball. _____

e. A woman is <u>jumping</u> into the swimming pool. _____

f. The girl with the helmet is <u>racing</u>. _____

g. <u>Three</u> runners are finishing the race. _____

4. Look at the bar graph. Complete the sentences. Use the *-ing* form of the verb.

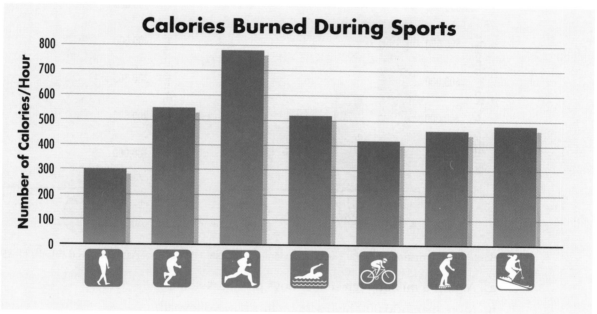

Based on information from: Sutcliffe, A. (ed.): *Numbers: How many, how far, how long, how much.*
(NY: HarperCollins, 1996)

a. _____Walking_____ burns 300 calories an hour.

b. _____ burns about 550 calories an hour.

c. According to the chart, _____ burns the most number of calories.

d. _____ burns the fewest number of calories.

e. _____ burns about 40 more calories an hour than riding a bike.

f. _____, skiing, and skating burn more calories than riding a bike but fewer calories than jogging.

5. What about you? Look at the chart in Exercise 4. Which activity would you most like to do? Why?

Example: *I'd like to swim because I love the water.*

Challenge Write five more sentences like the ones in Exercise 4.

Team Sports

1. Look at the basketball court in your dictionary. Write the numbers to complete these sentences.

   a. The referee is looking at player number ___7___ .

   b. The coach is pointing to players number _____ and number _____ .

   c. The home team's score is _____ .

2. Look at the bar graphs. **True** or **False**? Write a question mark (**?**) if the information isn't in the charts.

Most Popular High School Team Sports

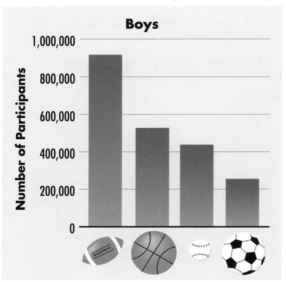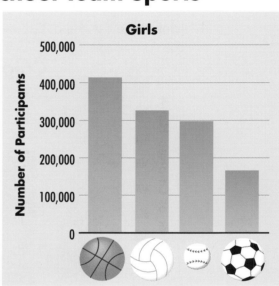

Based on information from the National Federation of State High School Associations (USA, 1993–1994)

   a. Almost a million high school boys play basketball.   ___False___

   b. More than 300,000 high school girls play volleyball.   _____

   c. Football is the most popular team sport among high school boys.   _____

   d. Soccer is the fourth most popular team sport for both girls and boys.   _____

   e. More than 200,000 boys play ice hockey.   _____

   f. More boys than girls play basketball.   _____

   g. Volleyball is less popular than softball among girls.   _____

   h. About 10,000 boys play water polo.   _____

   i. Baseball is more popular than soccer among boys.   _____

   j. More girls play softball than boys play baseball.   _____

3. What about you? Which sports would you prefer to play? Why? Use your own paper.

   a. baseball or softball   b. basketball or volleyball   c. soccer or football

   Example: *I'd prefer to play softball. It's less dangerous than baseball.*

Challenge Look at **page 186** in this book. Complete the chart.

1. Look in your dictionary. Cross out the word that doesn't belong. Give a reason.

a. billiards	~~track and field~~	golf	*It doesn't use a ball.*
b. fencing	gymnastics	wrestling	
c. archery	inline skating	skateboarding	
d. biking	horse racing	weightlifting	
e. bowling	martial arts	flying disc	

2. Look at the line graph. Circle the correct words to complete the sentences.

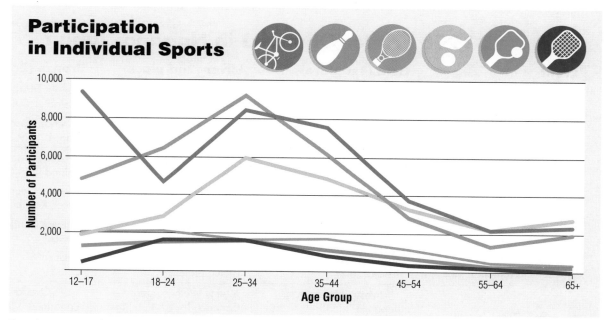

Based on survey of 10,000 homes by The National Sporting Goods Association (1994)

a. (Biking) / Bowling is the most popular sport for people 12 to 17 years old.

b. Racquetball / Table tennis is the least favorite sport for most age groups.

c. About the same number of people between the ages of 12 and 24 play racquetball / tennis.

d. Golf / Table tennis is the most popular sport for people over 65.

e. After the age of 45, golf / biking becomes more popular than bowling.

f. Between the ages of 12 and 24 participation in biking / bowling goes down.

g. Participation in racquetball / bowling goes down after age 34, but it goes up after age 64.

3. What about you? How has your participation in sports changed? Write sentences. Use your own paper.

Example: *I started to play more soccer in high school.*

Challenge Look at the chart in Exercise 2. Give possible reasons for some of the facts.

Winter Sports and Water Sports

1. Look in your dictionary. For which sports do you need…?

a. ice   <u>ice skating</u>   _____

b. wind   _____   _____

c. waves   _____

d. a motorboat   _____

e. mountains or hills   _____   _____   _____

f. a mask and fins   _____   _____

2. Look at the chart. Write the name of the sport to complete the sentences.

1998 Winter Olympics in Nagano, Japan

Event		Gold (1st place)	Silver (2nd place)	Bronze (3rd place)
	Men	Jean-Luc Cretier France 1:50.11	Lasse Kjus Norway 1:50.51	Hannes Trinkl Austria 1:50.63
	Women	Katja Seizinger Germany 1:28.89	Pernilla Wiberg Sweden 1:29.18	Florence Masnada France 1:29.37
	Men (10 km)	Bjorn Dahlie Norway 27:24.5	Markus Gandler Austria 27:32.5	Mika Myllylae Finland 27:40.1
	Women (10 km)	Larissa Lazutina Russia 46:06.9	Olga Danilova Russia 46:13.4	Katerina Neumannova Czech Republic 46:14.2
	Men	Ilya Kulik Russia	Elvis Stojko Canada	Philippe Candeloro France
	Women	Tara Lipinski United States	Michelle Kwan United States	Lu Chen China
	Men (500 m)	Hiroyasu Shimizu Japan 1:11.35	Jeremy Wotherspoon Canada 1:11.84	Kevin Overland Canada 1:11.86
	Women (500 m)	Catriona LeMay-Doan Canada 1:16.60	Susan Auch Canada 1:16.93	Tomomi Okazaki Japan 1:17.10
	Men	Ross Rebagliati Canada 2:03.96	Thomas Prugger Italy 2:03.98	Ueli Kestenholz Switzerland 2:04.08
	Women	Karine Ruby France 2:17.34	Heidi Renoth Germany 2:19.17	Brigitte Koeck Austria 2:19.42

a. Canada won four medals in the speed _____<u>skating</u>_____ event.

b. Russia won a gold and a silver medal in women's _____.

c. The United States won a gold and a silver medal in women's _____.

d. Austria won the bronze medal in the men's _____ event.

e. Thomas Prugger lost the gold medal in men's _____ by only .02 of a second.

f. _____ is not a timed event.

Challenge Which winter sports or water sports are best for where you live? Why?

1. Look in your dictionary. Which pieces of equipment are the customers talking about?

   a. "These are too heavy for me to lift." _____weights_____

   b. "Oh, I see them now. They're to the right of the bow." _____

   c. "There's one. Under the volleyball." _____

   d. "They look like ice skates with wheels." _____

   e. "Great! It's red and white—the same as my team's colors." _____

   f. "Well, this will really protect my head." _____

   g. "It would be fun to throw one of these around in the park. Nice colors, too." _____

   h. "Oh, there they are. Between the snowboard and the ski poles." _____

   i. "I have to wear them to protect my legs." _____

2. Look at the chart. Write comparisons with *more … than…*.

On an average day, Americans buy …

3,014   6,153   8,493   6,619   33,973

Based on information from: Heymann, T.: *On an Average Day.* (NY: Ballantine Books, 1989)

   a. soccer balls / basketballs   _They buy more basketballs than soccer balls._

   b. golf clubs / hockey sticks   _____

   c. tennis rackets / golf clubs   _____

   d. basketballs / tennis rackets   _____

3. What about you? Look in your dictionary. What would you buy from the store? Why?

   Example: *I'd buy a bat for my niece because she wants to play baseball.*

Challenge   Try to find the prices of these pieces of sports equipment. (Look at an ad, go to a sports store, or ask someone who knows.)

baseball glove _____   tennis racket _____   Other: _____ _____

Hobbies and Games

1. Look in your dictionary. Complete the crossword puzzle.

ACROSS →

1. It's not oil paint
5. It looks like a woman
7. It holds things together
8. Red, but not hearts
9. A board game
10. Black, but not spades
12. Type of paint
15. Type of game
16. You do this with needles
17. It's red, brown, yellow, and blue

DOWN ↓

2. It has a flower on it
3. These are cubes
4. You can collect these
6. You can build these
9. It's on the easel
11. Type of figure
13. You can collect these
14. You can make one from paper

2. Cross out the word that doesn't belong. Give a reason.

a.   checkers   chess   ~~crochet~~

It's not a board game.

b.   dolls   diamonds   clubs

_____

c.   watercolor   acrylic   clay

_____

d.   woodworking   yarn   doll making

_____

e.   cartridge   knitting needle   paintbrush

_____

3. Look at the bar graph. Circle the correct words to complete the sentences.

Playing Games (Last 2 Months)

Based on information from: Weiss, D. E.: *The Great Divide: How Females and Males Really Differ.* (NY: Poseidon Press, 1991)

a. In the last two months, women played more (cards)/ chess than men did.

b. Men played more cards / video games than any other type of game.

c. The smallest difference in percent of players was for checkers / chess.

d. The same percent of men played checkers and cards / chess.

e. Two percent fewer women played checkers / video games than men did.

4. Read the conversations. What are the people doing?

a. Amy: Six of diamonds.
Luis: Ten of clubs.   _playing cards_

b. Li-jing: That's nice yarn. What are you making?
Taro: A sweater for Hachi.   _____

c. Tommy: OK. Now I'll be an astronaut.
Nicki: And I'll be a woman from Mars.   _____

d. Min Ho: I found a 1963 penny.
Young Mee: And I found an old stamp.   _____

5. What about you? Check (✔) the things you collect.

☐ stamps   ☐ coins   ☐ baseball cards   ☐ figurines   ☐ Other: _____

Challenge Make a list of other things to collect. Ask your classmates for ideas.

Electronics and Photography

1. Look in your dictionary. What can you use to…?

a. wake up to music every morning   _clock radio_

b. watch television programs on a small screen   _____

c. keep photos neatly in one place   _____

d. listen to music while jogging   _____

e. record music from the radio   _____

f. change TV channels without getting up   _____

g. listen to music without anyone else hearing it   _____

h. listen to a news program from a country that is far away   _____

2. Look at the bar graph. Complete the sentences.

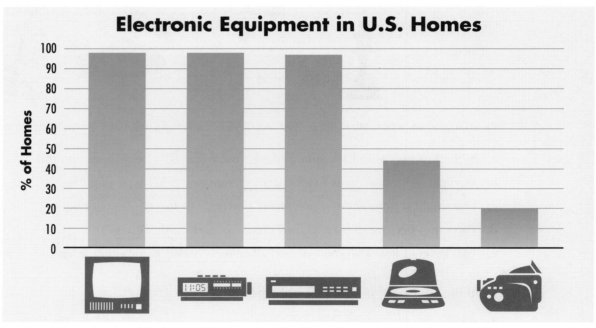

Based on information from: *The World Almanac and Book of Facts 1997.* (NJ: World Almanac Books, 1996)

a. Almost all U.S. homes have a _____ radio _____, a _____,

and a _____ .

b. Less than a quarter of the homes have a _____ .

c. A little less than half of the homes have a _____ .

d. Almost 55% more homes have a VCR than a _____ .

3. What about you? Look at the electronic equipment in Exercise 2. Which is the most important to you? Why?

_____

_____

4. Complete these instructions for a VCR.

Operation Buttons

a. _____Play_____ : to watch a tape

b. _____ : to move the tape backward

c. _____ : to stop the tape for a while during recording or playing

d. _____ : to tape a program (You must press PLAY at the same time.)

e. _____ : to stop playing or recording

f. _____ : to go to the end of the tape quickly

g. _____ : to take the videocassette out of the VCR

5. What's wrong with these pictures? Circle the words to complete the sentences.

a. The (photo) / slide is out of focus.

c. It's overexposed / underexposed .

b. She didn't use a camera case / tripod .

d. He didn't use a 35 mm camera / zoom lens .

Challenge Write instructions for using a cassette recorder, a clock radio, or another piece of electronic equipment.

Entertainment

1. Look in your dictionary. Where can you hear…?

   a. "Giddyap, Star. They're waiting for us back at the ranch." ____western____

   b. "And now a look at what's happening today in Europe." _____

   c. "It's Supercat, coming to save the world!" _____

   d. "Oops! Who put that banana peel there?" _____

   e. "A look at the score shows Bill leading by 98 points." _____

   f. "Bye, honey. Have a good day at the office." _____

   g. "Sir, tell our guest on stage what you think." _____

   h. "Don't be afraid. I come from a friendly planet." _____

   i. "And this beautiful necklace can be yours for just $39.95." _____

   j. "I love you and only you! Not your sister!" _____

   k. "Pandas live in the forests of central China." _____

   l.  _____ , _____ , or _____

2. Look at the chart. **True** or **False**? Write a question mark (?) if the information isn't there.

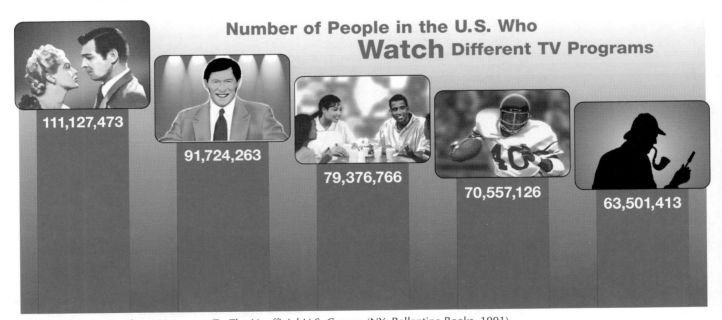

Number of People in the U.S. Who Watch Different TV Programs

111,127,473
91,724,263
79,376,766
70,557,126
63,501,413

Based on information from: Heymann, T.: *The Unofficial U.S. Census.* (NY: Ballantine Books, 1991)

   a. The most popular kind of program is the news. ____False____

   b. Sports programs are more popular than mysteries. _____

   c. More people watch sports programs than sitcoms. _____

   d. More than a hundred million people regularly watch movies on TV. _____

   e. Talk shows are as popular as news programs. _____

3. Circle the correct words to complete these movie listings.

MOVIE LISTINGS

ASTEROID ★★ (1997) Interesting made-for-TV mystery / (science fiction story) about an astronomer
a.
who works with the government to try to save the earth from a comet. With Michael Biehn and Annabella Sciorra. (2 hrs.) Sun 9 P.M. (Part 1) Ch 4

BIZET'S CARMEN ★★★★ (1984) Excellent film adaptation of the famous concert / opera by
b.
Georges Bizet, starring singers Julia Migenes-Johnson, Placido Domingo, and Jose Carreras. In French with English subtitles. (PG) (2½ hrs.) ART Sat 8 P.M.

HOME ALONE ★★★★ (1990) A very funny comedy / tragedy starring Macaulay Culkin about a
c.
family who accidentally goes on vacation without their eight-year-old son. Lots of laughs. (PG) (1¾ hrs.) ENS Sat 9 P.M.

JAWS ★★★★ (1975) A large shark terrorizes tourists at a local beach in this frightening horror story / romance directed by Steven Spielberg.
d.
You'll be scared out of your seat. (PG) (2 hrs.) TRE Sat 9 P.M.

THE LION KING ★★★★ (1994) Children and adults will love this full-length Disney cartoon / nature program which tells the story of
e.
baby Simba who will one day become king of the jungle. Great voices by James Earl Jones and Jeremy Irons. (G) (1½ hrs.) DIS Fri 7 P.M.

MISSION IMPOSSIBLE ★★★ (1996) Tom Cruise stars in this very exciting, fast-moving action adventure story based on the popular radio / television program watched by millions
f.
of people in the 1970s. (PG-13) (1¾ hrs.) DVS Fri 9 P.M.

THE TURNING POINT ★★★ (1977) Serious story of two dancers (Anne Bancroft and Shirley MacLaine) and the choices they make between family and career. Ballet / Mystery fans will love the
g.
beautiful dance scenes starring Mikhail Baryshnikov in his first film / play appearance. (PG) (2 hrs.)
h.
GEB Fri 9 P.M.

4. What about you? Look at the movie listings in Exercise 3. Which movie would you like to watch? Which movie wouldn't you like to watch? Why? Try to use the words *serious, funny, sad, boring,* and *interesting.*

_____

_____

Challenge Write two short reviews of television programs or movies. Give them a one- to four-star (★) rating.

1. Look in your dictionary. Complete these holiday cards.

a.
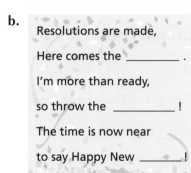
I looked real hard
to find this ___card___
just to say
on this special day—
That you're always a part
of my _____.
Happy _____

b.
Resolutions are made,
Here comes the _____ .
I'm more than ready,
so throw the _____ !
The time is now near
to say Happy New _____!

c.

As _____
light up the sky,
the red, white, and blue
will proudly fly!
Happy _____ !

d.
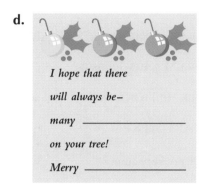
*I hope that there
will always be—
many* _____
on your tree!
Merry _____

e.

It's late November—
time to remember
To give thanks for
the good things this year
And, not the least,
A delicious _____
Where _____ and
stuffing appear.
Happy _____ !

f.

_____ burning bright
on a cool October night.
In scary costumes and a _____
for _____ treats
the children ask.
Happy _____ !

2. Look at the information. Complete the sentences.

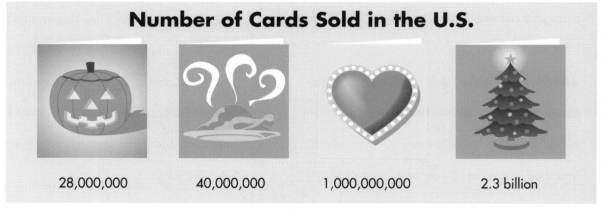

Number of Cards Sold in the U.S.

| 28,000,000 | 40,000,000 | 1,000,000,000 | 2.3 billion |

Based on information from: Droste, K. and J. Dye, (eds.): *Gale Book of Averages*. (MI: Gale Research, Inc., 1994)

a. The ____Halloween____ card has a picture of a jack-o'-lantern on it.

b. A billion cards are sold for _____ .

c. Americans buy the most number of cards for _____ .

d. The fewest number of cards are sold for _____ .

e. Twelve million more cards are sold for _____ than for Halloween.

Challenge Make a card for one of the holidays in your dictionary or for any other event.

1. Look in your dictionary. Complete Sue's letter. Use the past tense form of the verbs.

Dear Alicia,

Last night I went to Dave's house. When I got there, I rang the bell. As soon as Dave ___answered the door___ ,
a.
people jumped up and _____. They had
b.
been hiding behind the furniture! (And _I_ thought Dave and I were going to spend a quiet evening alone!) I was really surprised.

Dave _____ (8 of my classmates), and
c.
_____ with red, yellow, and blue balloons. He
d.
even baked a cake! It was beautiful. When it was time to eat it, Dave took a match and _____.
e.
Everyone _____ (in English!). Before
f.
I _____ (I was glad Dave only put
g.
eight in), I _____. Everyone asked what
h.
it was, but I didn't tell. After we had some cake, I
_____. And yours was there too!
i.
Thanks so much for the beautiful sweater. You
_____ the box so beautifully, too.
j.
Wish you could have been there with us.

Sue

2. What about you? Describe a party that you went to. Include as many details as possible. For example, what kind of party was it? Was it a surprise? How many guests were there? Was there a cake? Did people sing songs? Were there presents? Use your own paper.

Challenge Find out about birthday celebrations in other countries. Do people...?

sing songs   have a birthday cake   make a wish

blow out candles   give wrapped presents   open presents at the party

▶ Go to page 181 for Another Look (Unit 12).

Picture Comparison

Write about the two classrooms. How are they the same? How are they different?

Example: *Both of these classes are ESL classes. One class is ESL 101, the other class is ESL 102. Both classes have six students. In class 101, half the students are women, but in 102…*

A Picture Is Worth a Thousand Words

These are photographs by Alfred Eisenstaedt and other photographers. Write about the people in the photographs.

Alfred Eisenstaedt © Life Magazine, © Time Warner Inc.

Leonard Freed/Magnum

Describe the people.
What is their relationship?
Where are they?
What are they doing?
How do they feel?

Rondal Partridge/The Imogen Cunningham Trust

Bruno Barbey/Magnum

Word Map

Complete the diagram. Use the words in the box.

bathroom	bed	bedroom	blanket	~~children's bedroom~~
china cabinet	counter	dining area	drawer	dresser	end table
faucet	food processor	~~house~~	kitchen	lamp	living room
medicine cabinet	~~napkin~~	~~pillow~~	place mat	pot	~~rubber mat~~
set of dishes	shower	~~stereo system~~	~~stove~~	~~stuffed animal~~
table	toothbrush	~~toy chest~~	wall unit

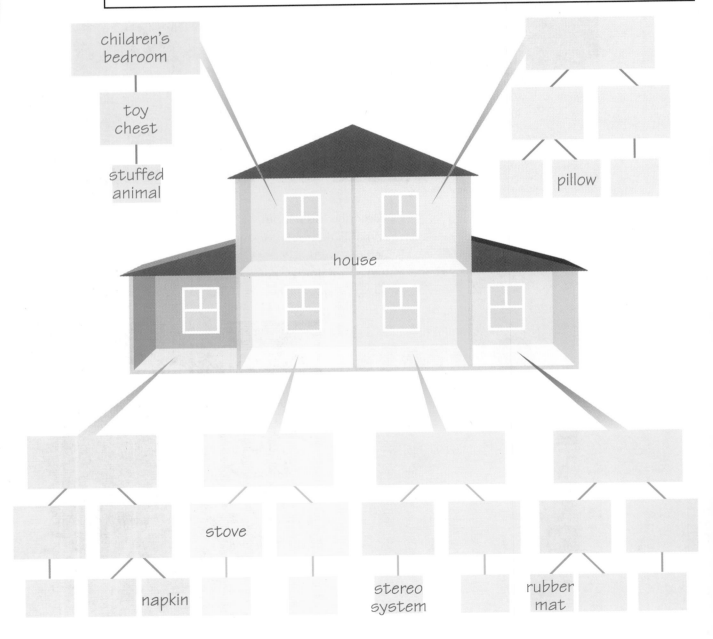

The Food Pyramid

In 1992 the U.S. government created the "food pyramid." It shows the types and amounts of food recommended daily for a healthy diet.

Look at the pyramid. There are 33 food words in it. The words go ➔ and ↓. Find and circle them. Then complete the food categories.

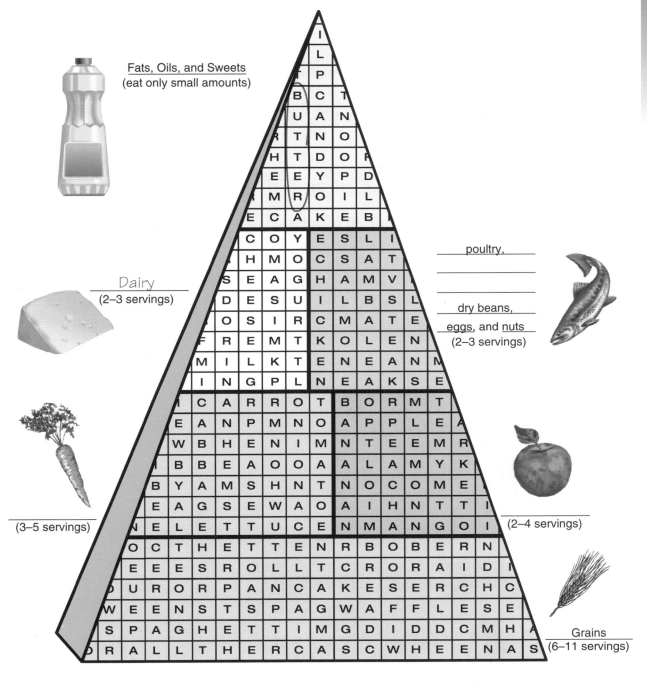

Fats, Oils, and Sweets
(eat only small amounts)

Dairy
(2–3 servings)

poultry, _____

_____

dry beans,

eggs, and nuts
(2–3 servings)

(3–5 servings)

(2–4 servings)

Grains
(6–11 servings)

List the categories and the foods that you circled. Add two foods to each category. Use your own paper.

Example: *Fats, Oils, and Sweets: butter,…*

Pack It Up!

You are going away for the weekend. What clothing and accessories would you take for each place? Put at least six items in each suitcase. You can use your dictionary for help.

WEEKEND FUN IN THE SUN!

Special 2-day package at The Sunshine Inn

2 bathing suits

Nature Club Overnight Trip

Fall Weekend
Meet: Sat. Sept 9, 7:00 A.M.

Rain or shine!

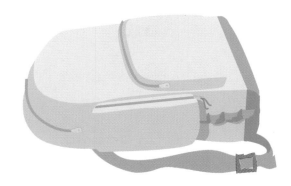

You are cordially invited to celebrate the marriage of

HEATHER MILLER TO BRIAN JOHNSON

at the
Country Manor Hotel Ballroom
Saturday, June 29, 8:00 P.M.

R.S.V.P.

CATSKILL SKI WEEKEND

Come join us for two days of fun and relaxation.

For further information: call 1-888-555-3421

Crossword Puzzle

Complete the puzzle.

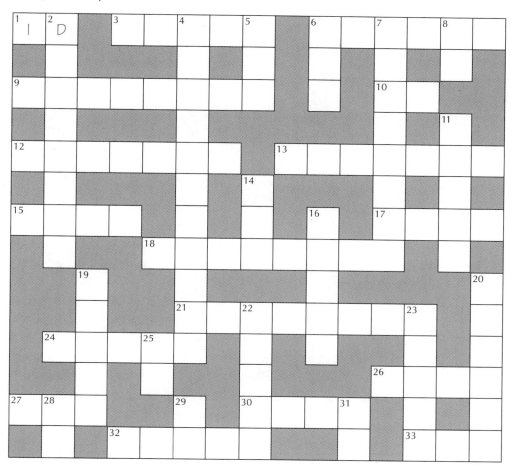

ACROSS ➡

1. Identification (short form)
3. _____ your teeth
6. A hole in a tooth
9. It holds your hair in place
10. Tuberculosis (short form)
12. Women wear it to smell good
13. You wash your hair with it
15. Your brain is inside it
17. Your throat is inside it
18. They help you walk
21. They operate on patients
24. Throw up
26. It holds gauze in place
27. It's part of the foot
30. _____-the-counter medication
32. Temperature
33. It has a lid

DOWN ⬇

2. A serious disease
4. An eye specialist
5. You do this with your eyes
6. Cardiopulmonary resuscitation (short form)
7. A, C, D, B$_6$, etc.
8. Listen _____ your heart
11. One of the five senses
14. You put a bandage on this
16. Part of your face
19. Break (past form)
20. You do this when you have a cold
22. You shave with this
23. You use this to find out your weight
25. Look _____ your throat
28. Put _____ sunscreen
29. Intravenous (short form)
31. Registered nurse (short form)

Things Change

Look at the maps of Middletown 50 years ago and Middletown today. What's different? What's the same? Write sentences. Use your own paper.

Example: *There was a bakery on the southeast corner of Elm and Grove. Now there's a coffee shop. There's still a…*

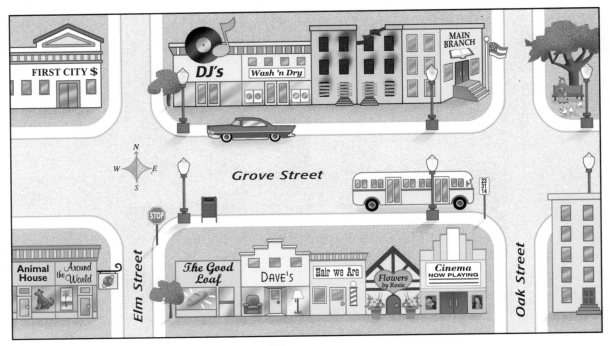

50 years ago

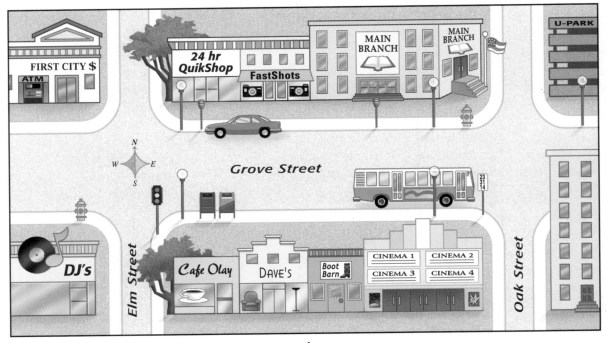

Today

What's Wrong With This Picture?

Look at the picture. Describe ten more problems. Use your own paper.

Example: *There's a plane flying under the bridge.*

Word Map

Complete the diagram. Use the words in the box.

~~addition~~	chemistry	civil rights	comma	desert
English composition	geography	guitar	high school	~~invention~~
lightbulb	magnet	~~math~~	mountain peak	mountain range
movement	multiplication	music	ocean	paper	paragraph
percussion	~~physics~~	~~piano~~	product	~~sand dune~~	science
~~sentence~~	strings	test tube	~~total~~	U.S. history

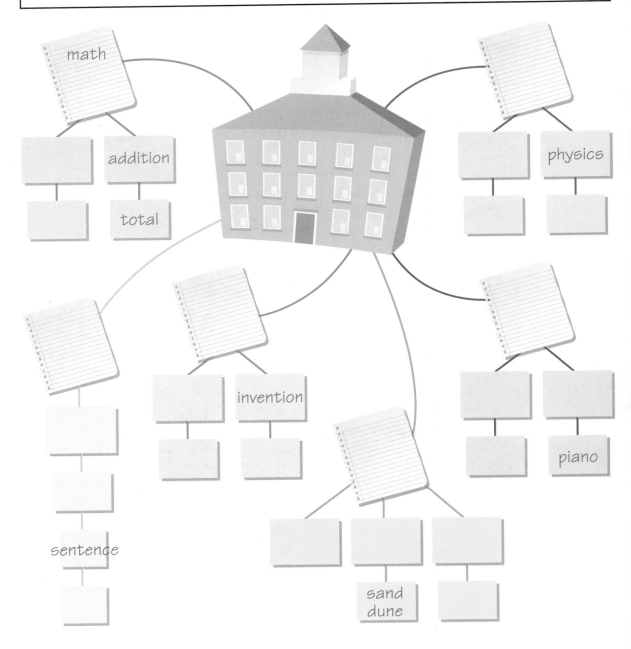

Word Search

There are 25 plant and animal words in the box. The words go ➡ and ⬇. Find and circle them.

L	I	O	N	P	A	R	O	S	E
L	C	A	T	I	R	O	O	E	L
A	D	K	O	N	A	O	C	A	E
M	O	N	K	E	Y	S	T	L	P
A	L	L	I	G	A	T	O	R	H
P	P	L	L	G	N	E	P	R	A
O	H	I	F	O	E	R	U	A	N
W	I	L	L	O	W	A	S	P	T
L	N	Y	Y	S	T	T	O	A	D
W	H	A	L	E	A	G	L	E	Y

Put the circled words into the correct categories.

FLOWERS	**SEA ANIMALS**	**AMPHIBIANS**	**INSECTS**
_____	_____	_____	_____
_____	_____	_____	_____

MAMMALS	**SEA MAMMALS**	**TREES AND PLANTS**	**BIRDS**
llama	_____	_____	_____
_____	_____	_____	_____
_____	_____	_____	_____
_____			_____

REPTILES	**RODENTS**
_____	_____

On the Job

Look at the pictures. Describe each photograph and answer the questions. Use your own paper.

a. Where are the people?

b. What are they doing?

c. What types of equipment are the people using?

d. What types of job skills do the people need to do these jobs?

e. How do you think the workers feel?

f. Compare the four jobs. How are they the same? How are they different?

g. Would you like to work in any of these places? Why or why not?

Crossword Puzzle

Complete the puzzle.

ACROS →

2. A water sport
4. Not funny
6. A type of paint
8. It goes up and down
11. You use them to light a campfire
14. Compact disc (short form)
15. Bucket
16. _____ and touch your toes
17. You see them in a theater
18. 35 _____ camera
19. Stand-_____ comedy
23. A bike with three wheels
25. You put a camera on it
26. Water at the beach
27. Run slowly

DOWN ↓

1. _____ a swing
2. A winter snow sport
3. _____ Year's Day
5. _____ crafts
7. _____ skating
9. New York 5, Los Angeles 3
10. Track and _____
12. Type of park
13. You can collect these
16. Dribble
20. Movie
21. You look at slides on it
22. Not interesting
23. You can sleep in it
24. Billiards

Challenge for page 9

How did you use the telephone last week? How many times did you...?

a. call collect _____

b. dial the wrong number _____

c. make an international call _____

d. call from a pay phone _____

e. use a phone card _____

f. call from a cellular phone _____

g. use directory assistance _____

h. use the telephone book _____

Challenge for page 10

Use the formulas to convert the temperatures. Then describe the temperature.

To convert Fahrenheit to Celsius:	**To convert Celsius to Fahrenheit:**
Subtract (−) 32, multiply (×) by 5, divide (÷) by 9	Multiply (×) by 9, divide (÷) by 5, add (+) 32
Example: 50°F = __?__ °C	Example: 25°C = __?__ °F
50−32 = 18 18×5 = 90 90÷9 = 10	25×9 = 225 225÷5 = 45 45+32 = 77
Answer: 50°F = 10°C	Answer: 25°C = 77°F

a. 25°C = _77°_ F ___warm___

b. 41°F = _____C _____

c. 68°F = _____C _____

d. 95°F = _____C _____

e. 30°C = _____F _____

f. −20°C = _____F _____

Challenge for page 17

Write six sentences comparing times in different cities. Use words, not numbers.

Example: *When it's five in the afternoon in Athens, it's eleven at night in Hong Kong.*

WHEN IT'S NOON EASTERN STANDARD TIME, IN... IT'S....					
Athens	7 P.M.	Hong Kong	1 A.M.*	Riyadh	8 P.M.
Baghdad	8 P.M.	Mecca	8 P.M.	St. Petersburg	8 P.M.
Bangkok	12 midnight	Mexico City	11 A.M.	San Juan	12 noon
Buenos Aires	2 P.M.	Paris	6 P.M.	Seoul	2 A.M.*
Halifax	1 P.M.	Rio de Janeiro	2 P.M.	Tokyo	2 A.M.*

* = morning of the next day

Challenge for pages 18–19

Add to the chart. Continue on your own paper if you need more space.

INTERNATIONAL HOLIDAYS		
DATE	**HOLIDAY**	**COUNTRY**
January 15	Adults Day	Japan
February 5	Constitution Day	Mexico
June 20	Flag Day	Argentina
July 14	Bastille Day	France
December 26	Boxing Day	Canada
_____	_____	_____
_____	_____	_____